BUSINESS the

Rupert Murdoch

Way

BUSINESS the

Rupert Murdoch

Way

10 Secrets of the World's Greatest Deal Maker

By Stuart Crainer

AMACOM

American Management Association

New York • Atlanta • Boston • Chicago • Kansas City • San Francisco • Washington, D.C.

Brussels • Mexico City • Tokyo • Toronto

This book is available at a special
discount when ordered in bulk quantities.
For information, contact Special Sales Department,
AMACOM, an imprint of AMA Publications, a division of
American Management Association,
1601 Broadway, New York, NY 10019.

Business the Rupert Murdoch Way was written independently by the author, Stuart Crainer. It has not been authorized by its subject.

This publication is designed to provide accurate and authoritative information in regard to the subject matter covered. It is sold with the understanding that the publisher is not engaged in rendering legal, accounting, or other professional service. If legal advice or other expert assistance is required, the services of a competent professional person should be sought.

Library of Congress Cataloging-in-Publication Data
Crainer, Stuart.
   Business the Rupert Murdoch way: ten secrets of the world's
  greatest deal maker / Stuart Crainer.
     p.   cm.
  Includes bibliographical references and index.
  ISBN 0-8144-7034-3
   1. Industrial management. 2. Murdoch, Rupert, 1931–   —Views on
industrial management. 3. Mass media—Management. I. Title.
HD31.C85   1999
658—dc21   98-50488
                                                   CIP

Published in North America by arrangement with Capstone
Publishing Limited, Oxford, United Kingdom.

Printing number

10 9 8 7 6 5 4 3 2 1

Contents

Five: King of the Nitty-Gritty   75
Murdoch knows his business inside out. News Corp
execs sleep uneasy. A 3 a.m. call from Murdoch checking on the figures is not unusual.

Six: DNA Marketing   85
Rupert Murdoch has marketing in his DNA. For him,
the hard sell is an instinct, an automatic impulse.

Seven: Speed Freaks   95
While other corporate behemoths take an age to make
a decision, entrepreneurial Murdoch is usually first to
the phone to clinch the deal.

Eight: Think Tomorrow Today   107
If you want to succeed in the future, you need to think
of tomorrow today. Murdoch bets on the future and
keeps his nerve as it unfolds.

Nine: Ambition Never Dies   119
Nearing seventy, Murdoch works like a man possessed.
He always wants more.

Ten: Drive the Company   129
Don't move and you will die. Keeping on moving is the
route to corporate success.

Preface

The management gurus tell us that in the contemporary business world learning is a source of competitive advantage. Managers must constantly learn new skills and techniques so that they are armed for corporate battle. Organizations must reinvent themselves as learning organizations in which learning is central to their being and culture. All this is no doubt true—in theory. But, in reality, there are few genuine learning organizations. The reality is that executives are not very good at learning. "Success in the marketplace increasingly depends on learning, yet most people don't know how to learn. What's more, those members of the organization that many assume to be the best at learning are, in fact, not very good at it," says Harvard Business School's Chris Argyris.[1] One of the aims of the Business Way series is to help executives learn by giving them the opportunity to learn from the best.

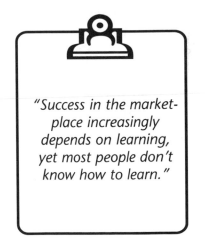

"Success in the marketplace increasingly depends on learning, yet most people don't know how to learn."

This may sound like an overly ambitious objective. But think how managers learn. First, they do so through experience. Yet, as Chris Argyris has pointed out, experience is no guarantee of learning. How many executives have you met who have all the experience in the world but little insight or real wisdom? They may proclaim that they have 30 years' experience, but they often have one year's experience 30 times. Experience does not automatically lead to learning. Years clocked up do not necessarily equate with wisdom.

The second source of learning for executives is training programs. Most senior managers have attended one business school executive program or another.

With their case studies and emphasis on the analytical, business schools undoubtedly enable managers to acquire important skills. But the range of skills and their practical usefulness is regularly questioned— not least by those who teach at business schools. "The idea that you can take smart but inexperienced 25-year-olds who have never managed anything or anybody and turn them into effective managers via two years of classroom training is ludicrous," says strategy guru Henry Mintzberg.[2]

The venerable Peter Drucker is another long-time critic of business schools. "The business schools in the U.S., set up less than a century ago, have been preparing well-trained clerks," he wrote as long ago as 1969.[3] More recently, he has predicted the decline of business schools, noting that "Business schools are suffering from premature success. Now, they are improving yesterday a little bit. The worst thing is to improve what shouldn't be done at all."

Business schools remain wedded to theory; business is about action. "I am not impressed by diplomas. They don't do the work. My marks were not as good as those of others, and I didn't take the final examination. The principal called me in and said I have to leave. I told him that I didn't want a diploma. They had less value than a cinema ticket. A ticket at least guaranteed that you would get in. A diploma guaranteed nothing," said Soichiro Honda, founder of Honda.[4]

Business schools remain wedded to theory; business is about action.

With surprising understatement, former Chrysler CEO Lee Iacocca noted: "Formal learning can teach you a great deal, but many of the essential skills in life are the ones you have to develop on your own." More opinionated was the late Avis chief and author of *Up the Organization*, Robert Townsend. "Don't hire Harvard Business School graduates," he warned. "This elite, in my opinion, is missing some pretty fundamental requirements for success: humility; respect for people in the firing line; deep understanding of the nature of the business and the kind of people who can enjoy themselves making it prosper; respect from way down the line; a demonstrated record of guts, industry, loyalty down, judgment, fairness, and honesty under pressure."[5]

More recently, Bill Gates, Virgin's Richard Branson and Body Shop's Anita Roddick have all been much quoted examples of those who missed out on business school but went on to reach the summits of business success. "A great advantage I had when I started the Body Shop was that I had never been to business school," says Anita Roddick. Similarly, 1-800-Flowers founder Jim McCann says that the company would have not got off the ground if he'd gone to business school—"I would have thought too much about why the deal couldn't be done," says McCann.[6]

The third source of learning is learning from peers and colleagues. This is very powerful. The current trend for mentoring and coaching is evidence that senior managers can play an important role in developing the skills of other, more junior, managers. But what if your boss is an ineffective time-server with no interest in developing tomorrow's talent? What if your boss is incompetent? What if your aspirations far outstrip the level of expertise of your boss? Who do you learn from then?

For many, the answer lies in the growing array of best-selling books by corporate leaders. Executives buy them by the millions. They want to know what makes a top CEO tick. They want it mapped out. Invariably they are disappointed. Most CEO-authored books are marred by ego and hindsight. They are ghostwritten and their merit is as illusory as a ghost. Most are rose-tinted celebrations of careers rather than objective examinations of managerial techniques. The learning they offer is limited—though that is not to deny the entertainment value.

The Business Way series aims to fill the gap. It seeks to give an objective view of the business practice and thinking of some of the corporate greats. For each of the business leaders in the series—whether it be Bill Gates, Rupert Murdoch, Richard Branson or Jack Welch—we look at the essence of their approach to business. What makes them different? What are they good at? And, most importantly, what lessons can be learned from their business success?

As you will see, the lessons aren't rocket science. Indeed, management is more pocket science. "Guru? You find a gem here or there. But most of it's fairly obvious, you know," says Rupert Murdoch. "You go to Doubleday's business section and you see all those wonderful titles and you spend $300 and then you throw them all away." Theory is for those with time on their hands. Making it happen is what management and business are all about.

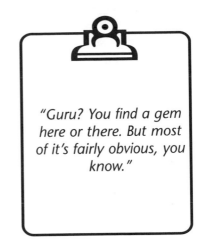

"Guru? You find a gem here or there. But most of it's fairly obvious, you know."

NOTES

1 Argyris, Chris, "Teaching smart people how to learn," *Harvard Business Review*, May–June 1991.

2 Mintzberg, Henry, "The new management mind-set," *Leader to Leader*, Spring 1997.

3 Drucker, Peter, *The Age of Discontinuity*, Heinemann, London, 1969.

4 Crainer, Stuart (editor), *The Ultimate Book of Business Quotations*, Capstone, Oxford, 1997; AMACOM, New York, 1998.

5 Townsend, Robert, *Up the Organization*, out of print.

6 Bruce, Katherine, "How to succeed in business without an MBA," *Forbes*, January 26, 1998.

BUSINESS the
Rupert
murdoch
Way

The Life and Times of Rupert Murdoch

S ome hugely successful executives are lauded as popular heroes. Ex-Chrysler chief Lee Iacocca and Virgin's Richard Branson fit into this category. They write books, sit on the right committees, work for charity and appear approachable, not quite ordinary, but kind of normal. Some, Jack Welch perhaps, are quietly admired as astute but not particularly lovable. Others are beyond the pale, not the kind of people you would like to have around for dinner—people like downsizer Al Dunlap. And yet, doubted, distrusted and plain disliked though they may be, they are hugely successful.

The Australian media tycoon Rupert Murdoch clearly falls into the final category. He is viewed by some with deep suspicion; others regard him with fear and loathing (usually in about equal measure). Others laud his business acumen, his ability to get the prize, his global business empire. He is a man on whom virtually all have an opinion. Keith Rupert Murdoch—

KRM to his employees—is probably the most famous businessperson in the world, whose power and influence are only matched by his profits and ambition. The *Washington Post* has called him "the global village's de facto communications minister."[1]

Elsewhere, Murdoch has been labeled "the media's demon king." The British satirical magazine, *Private Eye*, calls him the Dirty Digger (though this is preferable to what it calls a number of others). And that other media mogul, Ted Turner, has, in court depositions, called Murdoch a "slimy character" and "a dangerous person." (Turner's ire was aroused when the Murdoch-owned *New York Post* ran an unflattering article on his wife, Jane Fonda. More recently, Turner has suggested that the two climb into a boxing ring to resolve their differences. The pay-per-view possibilities are endless.) Mike Royko, the Chicago columnist, colorfully described Murdoch as a "greedy, money-grubbing, power-seeking, status-climbing cad."[2] Messrs. Turner and Royko are probably not on the Murdoch family's Christmas card list.

More moderate voices become excited at the mention of the M word. British politician Lord Hattersley, neither a mogul nor a satirist, called Murdoch a "tycoon who is a danger to our democracy."[3] Another peer, Lord McNally, simply noted that "What is good business for Murdoch is not necessarily good sense for a healthy democracy or a diverse and healthy press." The English *Independent on Sunday* newspaper observed that "In a previous century, he would have been one of the American robber barons" and that "Trying to stop him being predatory is like trying to turn a vulture into a vegetarian."[4] Along similar lines, an American magazine noted: "Mr. Murdoch is aggressive: he makes media tycoons like Ted Turner and John Malone look like boy scouts."[5]

For a media master, Murdoch has certainly had bad press. (A few words in his defense come from Los Angeles Mayor Richard Riordan who called him "a very quality human being."[6] Murdoch was also one of three non-Catholics to receive the honorary title of Knight Commander of St. Gregory the Great in January 1998, an award for "unblemished character" from the Catholic Church. Perhaps they know something the rest of the world does not.)

"Trying to stop him being predatory is like trying to turn a vulture into a vegetarian."

While Rupert Murdoch has been demonized— and sometimes lionized as king of the corporate chieftains—what is clear is that he is a man few appear to understand to any degree. Even his biographer, the inquisitive and astute William Shawcross, failed to penetrate Murdoch's carefully constructed carapace of privacy and mystery—though he did conclude that Murdoch was "one of the most powerful men on earth."[7]

EARLY LIFE

What can be said is that Rupert Murdoch was born in Australia in 1931. He has referred to the early institutions that "formed" him as Toorak Presbyterian Church (his grandfather preached there sometimes);

Geelong Grammar School; and Flemington Race Course. Their influence was not necessarily felt in that order.

> *"He contains within his character both an extraordinary gambling instinct and a certain dour puritanism."*

Murdoch's parents had a strong influence on his life. This is a trite statement and in most cases, it is an easy but largely incorrect statement. In Rupert Murdoch's case it is entirely accurate. From his father, Sir Keith Murdoch, Rupert inherited his love of business and, in particular, of the newspaper business. The Murdoch side of the family were keen members of the Free Church of Scotland. From his mother, Dame Elisabeth, Murdoch inherited a fiery determination and a love of risk taking. "He contains within his character both an extraordinary gambling instinct and a certain dour puritanism," noted William Shawcross. Both have stood him in good stead.

Rupert was educated at Geelong Grammar and during his school holidays worked at the offices of the *Melbourne Herald* where his father worked. He was then dispatched to England in 1950 to go to Oxford University's Worcester College.

This proved a mixed experience for the young Murdoch. The Britain of the early 1950s was still suffering from a postwar hangover as well as the usual un-Melbourne-like weather. "I vividly recall the rationing, the queues, the shortages, the shabbiness, the general weariness," Murdoch said in 1994.[8] Murdoch studied economics and graduated in 1952. He then worked on Fleet Street (then in its heyday as the hub of the British newspaper industry) as a sub-editor at Lord Beaverbrook's *Daily Express*.

Rupert followed doggedly and deliberately in his father's footsteps. Sir Keith Murdoch was a traditional newspaperman. His formative experience in the newspaper industry came when he arrived in London in 1915 fresh from the carnage of Gallipoli. The Australian worked with Lord Northcliffe, who provided lifelong inspiration to him—and later to his son. Sir Keith was inspired by Lord Northcliffe's success with the *Daily Mail*. Launched in 1896, the newspaper tapped into a new mass market with its brand of populism. Northcliffe's slogan for it was "The busy man's paper." Large and cigar-smoking, Northcliffe was said to possess "the common mind to an uncommon degree." His first great triumph was when he ran a competition in his publication *Answers* to guess the amount of gold in the Bank of England on a particular day. The prize of £1 a day for life attracted 718,218 hopeful entries.

Northcliffe later visited Sir Keith Murdoch in Melbourne where Murdoch was editor of the *Melbourne Herald*. "He seems to have a great knowledge and to be simple and direct in his purposes," said Sir Keith of Northcliffe. "That, I think, is the secret of his success, if he can claim true success. He knows what he wants and goes straight for it."[9] Northcliffe's approach was enthusiastically emulated by both Sir Keith and his son.

Rupert Murdoch has said that Northcliffe's insistence on lots of news and a balance between editorial coverage and advertising influenced him—though Northcliffe's gift for dreaming up circulation-boosting competitions probably did not escape his notice. "I think there's no doubt that the type of mass popular journalism that Northcliffe brought to newspapers has now extended to television," he said in a 1994 lecture—going on to note that Northcliffe also went mad.[10]

Murdoch on Northcliffe:

"The type of mass popular journalism that Northcliffe brought to newspapers has now extended to television."

In 1952 Rupert inherited the *Adelaide News* and *Sunday Mail* from his father. Sir Keith had had misgivings about whether his son would make the grade. According to Dame Elisabeth, Rupert's "father was somewhat critical of Rupert as a young man and questioned whether he had it in him to take over the company."

Even so, Sir Keith Murdoch's will stated: "I desire that my said son Keith Rupert Murdoch should have the great opportunity of spending a useful, altruistic and full life in newspaper and broadcasting activities and ultimately occupying a position of high responsibility in that field." Not surprisingly, amateur psychologists usually conclude that the father–son relationship is crucial to any understanding of Murdoch's motivation and success.

The *Adelaide News*, as left by Sir Keith Murdoch, was an uninspiringly small newspaper. The Murdoch inheritance was no empire. To it, Rupert brought youthful vigor and a willingness to embrace the mass market. This he did with Northcliffe-like enthusiasm. "Queen Eats a Rat" was one of his more sensational headlines. Rupert had the advantage—or disadvantage—of being thrown in at the deep end at an early age. While others progressed up a hierarchy, Murdoch made his own mistakes and mastered management alone while still a young man. Perhaps this is the first secret of his success—early responsibility, the opportunity to learn and to make mistakes.

Murdoch took to business life easily. His life had been a preparation for it. From the very start, Murdoch began stretching his wings. As the ink dried and the presses whirled, deals were struck. In 1960, Murdoch bought the Sydney *Daily Mirror* and tested the water in the television market. Various deals came and went. Murdoch later explained the rationale behind his apparently indiscriminate purchasing: "We tended to take the sick newspapers, the ones that weren't worth much, that people thought were about to fold up."[11] The purchases were backed by borrowing. Murdoch quickly learned that banks were only concerned about how reliably clients repaid their loans. Murdoch established a record of doing what he promised. Banks rolled over and offered more.

Perhaps the boldest sign of Murdoch's broadening ambitions was his founding of *The Australian*, the country's first national newspaper. Promising "to report the nation to Canberra and Canberra to the nation," *The Australian* started life in 1964. What marked it apart from Murdoch's other ventures of the time was that it was a broadsheet with a heavier agenda (as well as a greater capacity to lose money). Firmly on its agenda was political power. *The Australian* placed Murdoch at the center of power. He became a national figure. Though the newspaper lost money for years (broadsheet equals unpopular in Murdoch's terminology) it made a mark. "He started to think of himself as somebody who could perhaps take part in the making and unmaking of governments, particularly unmaking I think," former political reporter Mungo MacCullum commented in a later TV program.[12]

NEW HORIZONS

By the late 1960s, Murdoch's Australian interests were many and varied. He began to look further afield. The first international deal that shaped the media image of Murdoch was the purchase of the British Sunday newspaper, the *News of the World,* in 1969. The *News of the World* was downmarket and addictively populist long before Murdoch entered the newspaper business. It was not known as "The news of the screws" for nothing.

The *News of the World* was owned by the Carr family, who held 27 percent of the company shares. Unfortunately for them, a quarter of the company's shares were in the hands of a family cousin who wanted out. First on the scene to buy the shares was Robert Maxwell, whose career was to shadow Murdoch's for the next 20 years.

"This is a British newspaper, run by British people. Let's keep it that way."

Maxwell was not a welcome suitor. He was everything the Carrs detested. Unpleasant nationalism quickly surfaced. On October 20, 1968, the *News of the World* editor, Stafford Somerfield, characteristically pontificated: "Why do I think that it would not be a good thing for Mr. Maxwell, formerly Jan Ludwig Hoch, to gain control of this newspaper which, I know, has your respect, loyalty and affection—a newspaper which I know is as British as roast beef and Yorkshire pudding? . . . This is a British newspaper, run by British people. Let's keep it that way." (Murdoch later said that Somerfield was an editor he had admired.)

The roast beef defense is always a sign of desperation among the British. But for the Carr family these were desperate times. "That foreigner" is how the Carrs described Maxwell. The trouble for them was that there weren't any members of the British aristocracy willing to stump up the cash for their saucy scandal sheet. Their unlikely knight in shining armor was Rupert Murdoch. Somehow, the Australian was deemed less foreign than Maxwell, who had lived in the country for decades, been an MP and won the Military Cross.

Blind prejudice gave Murdoch an intro into international newspaper publishing. The British Establishment closed ranks against Maxwell and welcomed Murdoch as an honorary member. Murdoch played his part brilliantly. He wined and dined. He smoothed a potentially difficult path. The Carrs felt reassured. Murdoch's masterly move was to ask Sir William Carr to remain as chairman with his nephew as joint managing director with Murdoch. The deal was made on the premise that the Carr involvement in the newspaper would continue.

The prize was won at an Extraordinary General Meeting at the Connaught Rooms near London's Covent Garden on January 2, 1969. Maxwell told Murdoch that he had caught "a big fish with a very small hook."[13] For once, Maxwell was not exaggerating. Murdoch could not have afforded to match Maxwell's offer and it was only through various exchanges of shares that the deal was possible. The Carrs actually lost around £2 million in accepting their knight in shining armor rather than Maxwell. For Murdoch it was a lucky break. It was the deal he needed to make the leap from national newspaper proprietor to international media kingpin. His orbit of influence expanded overnight.

Soon after, Murdoch wrote to Sir William Carr informing him that the joint managing director arrangement was not tenable and a new chairman would also be a good idea. And, after promising not to seek to own the newspaper outright, six months later Murdoch sought control, buying the shares of the Carrs' cousin.

The *News of the World* was only the starter. It was a Sunday newspaper. The archaic inefficiency of Fleet Street meant that the presses remained silent during the week. It made obvious sense to use them.

And so, Murdoch rolled out a brash new form of populist journalism with the purchase for less than £500,000 of another British newspaper, the *Sun*, in 1969. To some the *Sun* was—and still is—the summation of all that is wrong with Murdoch. It is resolutely downmarket, famed for its Page Three topless models, pithy tastelessness, gung-ho nationalism and insatiable interest in the comings and goings of the stars. "He [Murdoch] regarded journalism really as a branch of the entertainment business and he thought that people bought a paper not to be instructed or

"He regarded journalism really as a branch of the entertainment business."

edified or to know about the world, but to have a world," commented British columnist Alan Watkins. Watkins was right. No one, at that time, actually regarded newspapers as entertainment—and if they did, they were generally doing a remarkably bad job at providing it.

Thirty years on, the *Sun* and the *News of the World* remain highly lucrative parts of Murdoch's corporate empire, assembled under the News Corporation name. (In 1997 News Corp reported that the *News of the World* had an average circulation of 4.5 million, while the *Sun* claimed to have over 10 million readers every single day.) Others soon followed. Among them was the *New York Post,* bought by Murdoch in 1976. His relationship with the *Post* has been a typically complex saga. He lost control of it in 1988—because he bought a local TV station, WNYW—and then regained control in 1993 when the newspaper was acquired once again by News Corp.

FIGHTING BATTLES

In 1981, Murdoch launched a remarkable new chapter in his career when he bought the (London) *Times,* fighting off bids from the newspaper's editor (William Rees-Mogg) and a group of journalists, as well as from the editor of the *Sunday Times,* Harold Evans, and the inevitable Robert Maxwell. The "top people's paper" was an unlikely bedfellow for the *Sun.* Indeed, with its court circulars and overbearing sense of tradition, the *Times* was an unlikely bedfellow for any other newspaper. There were predictable gasps of amazement when Murdoch, the downmarket populist, bought the bastion of English journalism. There were various pronouncements of impending doom and elderly clergy turned the pages with new excitement, anticipating the arrival of their very own Page Three girl.

The purchase of the *Times* marked another important threshold in Murdoch's career. It was, after all, the newspaper of the Establishment that Murdoch expressed his distaste for. Then Murdoch found himself waging war on behalf of the Establishment.

Murdoch's newspapers in the U.K. were profitable. But with growing interests elsewhere, he was keen to maximize their profit potential. Cash cows have to be milked. Blocking his path were the undoubtedly outdated processes and unions of Fleet Street. Demarcations and closed shops meant that the unions had a stranglehold on how and where newspapers were produced. Proprietors had gone along with these arrangements for decades. (It should not be forgotten that they, too, were culpable for the resulting inefficiencies and extravagances.) Murdoch drove a bulldozer through them.

In Wapping, in the East of London, he built a new printing plant that didn't need union labor. Computers were installed, which meant that editorial content could be transferred directly to the page. On January 25, 1986 four million newspapers were produced at Wapping. This precipitated war.

Over the following months, Wapping became a battlefield. Thousands of pickets, from the print unions and others, attempted to bring printing at the plant to an end. The protests were increasingly violent and raged throughout most of 1986. The end result was complete victory for Murdoch. The printers were paid off with £60 million and disappeared into history. Murdoch was left with a massively more efficient operation and substantially reduced costs. Valuations of News Corp soared from $300 million to $1 billion.

Murdoch's confrontation with the unions was a defining moment in his career, in the history of the unions and in British culture in the 1980s. It was also the defining moment in the public's perception of Murdoch. He was shown to be decisive and ruthless, someone who got what he wanted. He was clearly not only a powerful man but someone who was intent on using his power to create a business empire.

During the 1980s, Murdoch created his empire. Acquisition followed acquisition. His aspirations appeared ever bolder. In 1985 he acquired Fox Studios; seven Metromedia TV stations followed in 1986; and, in 1988, he paid Walter Annenberg $3.2 billion for *TV Guide*.

TURNING POINTS

1969   *The Lucky Break: Murdoch buys the* News of the World *for less than the price offered by Robert Maxwell. A combination of shrewd financing, wining and dining, and cunning, wins the day.*

1986   *The Battle: Murdoch overcomes the power of the unions in the British newspaper industry. He drags the industry into the twentieth century, makes it enormously more viable and potentially profitable, and opens up new markets.*

1990   *The Debt Crisis: Weighed down with enormous debts, News Corp is almost brought to its knees. Murdoch scrapes together a saving deal.*

The spending flurry was impressive but it was built on a mountain of debt that made Robert Maxwell look the very model of financial prudence. The beginning of the 1990s marked a watershed. News Corp's fabulous debts—$7 billion and counting—nearly brought it to its knees. Only a last-minute deal at the beginning of 1991 saved Murdoch's empire from ignominious collapse.

Undaunted, Murdoch has refused to stand still. During the 1990s, Murdoch's ambitions have expanded upward. His deals have become more global and distant from his newspaper roots.

In 1993 he revived the *New York Post* from bankruptcy; then he bought 63.3 percent of Star TV, the Hong Kong satellite network covering Asia, as well as snatching the NFL broadcasting rights from CBS. A relentless pace has been maintained. Saluting Murdoch as one of the titans in its Elite 100 for 1997, *Upside* magazine reviewed a year in Murdoch's whirlwind: "Murdoch cracked the xenophobic Japanese TV market, starting Japan Sky Broadcasting with Softbank (Sony and Fuji Television climbed onboard later as equal partners). News Corp purchased Heritage Media Corp for $754 million, Murdoch ruthlessly dumped EchoStar to buy Primestar, and he put a down payment on his halo when he picked up Pat Robertson's angelic International Family Entertainment for $1.9 billion. Murdoch outdid himself again, building the first truly integrated news-media empire." Just another year. *Upside* missed a few of Murdoch's other activities. Fox Sports *Américas* was launched in Latin America; Fox News Channel was launched, aiming to reach over 40 million households by 2000; News Corp acquired New World Communications; satellite services were launched in Brazil and Mexico; *Independence Day* was a hit movie; and the *Times* launched a price war.

Month after month, the deals keep coming. Look at Murdoch's headline-making deals during a mere six months in 1998:

♦ March 1998: Bought the LA Dodgers baseball team for $300 million (the previous record paid was $173 million for the Baltimore Orioles).

♦ April 1998: Acquired distribution rights to the new series of *Star Wars* films.

♦ June 1998: Sold the 13-million-circulation *TV Guide* to TCI's Universal Video Satellite Group for $2 billion.

♦ July 1998: Murdoch announced that he was floating off 20 percent of Fox group to help reduce News Corp's debts of $6.5 billion.

The end result is a personal wealth now calculated at many billions of dollars—anything from $3 billion to $10 billion depending on what you believe. Murdoch's is a truly global empire—according to *Asia Week*, Murdoch is the fourth most powerful person in Asia. The total assets of News Corp (as of March 1998) were $33.2 billion and the company had total annual revenues of US$13 billion.[14] The News Corp empire includes BSkyB, News International, the Los Angeles Dodgers, HarperCollins, Twentieth Century Fox, Fox TV, Star TV and many more, over 780 businesses in 52 countries. It is a huge global business empire that brought us *Titanic* and *The Simpsons* as well as delivering a daily diet of scurrilous gossip. News Corp not only owns many companies, it has shares in many other ventures. These crisscross the earth and cross political affiliations. For example, News Corp has invested in ChinaByte, a joint venture with the *People's Daily* newspaper in China. "No company in the world can match News Corporation in its ability to maximize its own product across multiple distribution platforms around the world," says Murdoch.[15]

In 1997 Murdoch quietly announced that the Murdoch family stake in News Corp now belonged to his children. While the Murdoch family owns 36.2 percent of the company, it is, to all intents and purposes, Rupert Murdoch's company. News Corp is Murdoch's corporate empire—and what an empire.

MURDOCH'S WORLD

Technology

Delphi Internet Services

Etak Inc.

Fox Interactive

HarperCollins News Media

Kesmai Corp

News Electronic Data

Entertainment

Fox Broadcasting Network

Fox Television Stations (22 stations)

Fox News Channel

Fox Sports Net (part owner)

Family Channel (part owner)

F/X (cable TV)

SF Broadcasting
Twentieth Century Fox
Twentieth Television
BSkyB (part owner)
British Sky Broadcasting (part owner)
Star Television
Los Angeles Dodgers

Publishing

HarperCollins
Mirabella
The Times Literary Supplement

Newspapers

New York Post
Weekly Standard (Washington, D.C.)
News of the World (U.K.)
The Sun (U.K.)
The Sunday Times (U.K.)
The Times (London)
Sydney Sunday & Daily Telegraph (Australia)
Melbourne Herald Sun (Australia)

THE 10 KEY MANAGEMENT SKILLS
OF RUPERT MURDOCH

Forget the mythology. The reality is that Rupert Murdoch is not the demon portrayed by much of the media. He is a highly successful businessman. (It is also worth remembering that the media pundits who write

about him usually work for his direct competitors.) Strangely, though he sits atop one of the world's most successful and influential businesses, there has been little research into his managerial style. There have been books and profiles of Murdoch the man, but very little is known of him as a manager.

There are a number of reasons for this. First, there is the temptation to believe in the mythology of Murdoch the ogre. This depicts Murdoch as a traditional, dictatorial newspaper proprietor in the Hearst or Northcliffe mold. *Citizen Kane* has a lot to answer for. This is management by exercise of power rather than the exercise of more subtle skills. Obviously, Rupert Murdoch uses all the power and influence at his disposal, but there is more to his managerial style than that. Managing a massive, dispersed organization at the leading edge of technology requires sophisticated management. Brute force and belligerence only get you so far.

The second reason why Murdoch and News Corp have been generally ignored by serious students of management is snobbery. Murdoch is no business school intellectual. He despises the "Establishment"— even though he is now effectively part of the Establishment. (As we have seen, his first major international break—the purchase of the *News of the World*— actually came about because he was the Establishment figurehead against the anti-Establishment Maxwell.) He is an outsider—or likes to think of himself as such. Murdoch is seen as beyond the pale.

Managing a massive, dispersed organization at the leading edge of technology requires sophisticated management.

The first accusation leveled against Murdoch is that he is morally reprehensible, king of the down-market tabloids, willing to play to the lowest common denominator of human behavior. The second concern is that it is dangerous for so much media power to be concentrated in the hands of one individual.

There is truth in both accusations. The *Sun* and Murdoch's other tabloids are resolutely downmarket. Murdoch, however, would retort that he is merely responding to public demand. The public gets what the public wants.

On the question of media power he is dismissive, pointing out that state monopolies have far greater influence. "If unhealthy concentration does exist today, it exists not in the private sector but with state broadcasting," Murdoch told a 1998 conference. To Murdoch, he is simply playing within the rules—playing hard, but breaking no laws or regulations. The free market is his mantra and get-out clause—"Because capitalists are always trying to stab each other in the back, free markets do not lead to monopolies. Essentially, monopolies can only exist when governments support them."[16]

Arguments about his pursuits will continue to rage so long as Murdoch is in business. What they usually do not recognize is the managerial ability that lies behind his success. In the pantheon of management greats of our time, Murdoch is unique. Other industrialists, such as Bill Gates, are not celebrated for their management

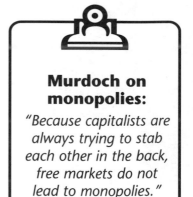

Murdoch on monopolies:

"Because capitalists are always trying to stab each other in the back, free markets do not lead to monopolies."

style but for their timing and innovative powers. Others have built their success on one great, ground-breaking product or service.

Rupert Murdoch is unique because his success has been based on great management. Compare, for example, Murdoch's performance against the competencies required of managers:

In *The Nature of Managerial Work*, the esteemed Canadian academic and author Henry Mintzberg identifies the characteristics of the manager at work:

- Performs a great quantity of work at an unrelenting pace.
- Undertakes activities marked by variety, brevity and fragmentation.
- Has a preference for issues that are current, specific and non-routine.
- Prefers verbal rather than written means of communication.
- Acts within a web of internal and external contacts.
- Is subject to heavy constraints but can exert some control over the work.

From these observations, Mintzberg identified the manager's "work roles" as:

Interpersonal roles

- Figurehead: representing the organization or unit to outsiders
- Leader: motivating subordinates, unifying effort
- Liaiser: maintaining lateral contacts

Informational roles

+ Monitor: of information flows
+ Disseminator: of information to subordinates
+ Spokesperson: transmission of information to outsiders

Decisional roles

+ Entrepreneur: initiator and designer of change
+ Disturbance handler: handling non-routine events
+ Resource allocator: deciding who gets what and who will do what
+ Negotiator: negotiating

"All managerial work encompasses these roles, but the prominence of each role varies in different managerial jobs," writes Mintzberg.[17] Murdoch has proved himself a master of virtually all these roles. He is an inveterate networker both inside and outside News Corp; a master of acquiring and retaining information; and entrepreneurial in both outlook and behavior. In addition, Murdoch is a model of the manager as insatiable dealmaker.

Clearly, Murdoch's approach and situation are unique. Seeking to emulate Murdoch is a dangerous thing to do—as his children may well find out if they seek to do so. Even so, lessons can be learned from his career and approach to doing business.

The key management lessons from Rupert Murdoch's career are:

1. **Go with the Flow.** Only the pragmatic survive in the corporate war zone. Rupert Murdoch is the ultimate chameleon.

2. **Goodbye, Mr. Nice Guy.** Nice guys finish second. In the world of Rupert Murdoch, ruthlessness is expected; weakness leads to corporate Siberia.

3. **Place Your Bets.** Rupert Murdoch is a gambler. He thrives on risks and the bigger the stakes, the bigger the buzz and the bigger the payout.

4. **Lead from the Front.** Murdoch is News Corporation. Forget ideas about empowerment. Flim-flam. Get up and lead.

5. **King of the Nitty-Gritty.** Murdoch knows his business inside out. News Corp execs sleep uneasy. A 3 a.m. call from Murdoch checking on the figures is not unusual.

6. **DNA Marketing.** Rupert Murdoch has marketing in his DNA. For him, the hard sell is an instinct, an automatic impulse.

7. **Speed Freaks.** While other corporate behemoths take an age to make a decision, entrepreneurial Murdoch is usually first to the phone to clinch the deal. News Corp is a dynamic organization—despite its size.

8. **Think Tomorrow Today.** If you want to succeed in the future, you need to think of tomorrow today. Murdoch bets on the future and keeps his nerve as it unfolds.

9. **Ambition Never Dies.** Nearing seventy, Murdoch works like a man possessed. He always wants more.

10. **Drive the Company.** Don't move and you will die. Keeping on moving is the route to corporate success.

NOTES

1 Farhi, Paul, "Loopholes boost Murdoch's profits," *Washington Post*, December 7, 1997.

2 Farhi, Paul, "Murdoch, all business," *Washington Post*, February 12, 1995.

3 "Blair's red-top baron," *Independent on Sunday*, February 15, 1998.

4 "Blair's red-top baron," *Independent on Sunday*.

5 Gove, Alex, "Lord of the skies," *Red Herring*, Issue 44, July 1997.

6 "O'Malley and Murdoch reported close to deal," *Los Angeles Times*, May 13, 1997.

7 Shawcross, William, *Murdoch*, Chatto & Windus, London, 1992.

8 Murdoch, Rupert, "The century of networking," The 11th Annual John Bonython Lecture, Melbourne, Australia, October 20, 1994.

9 Shawcross, William, *Murdoch*.

10 Murdoch, Rupert, "The century of networking."

11 *Detroit News*, November 7, 1995.

12 "Who's afraid of Rupert Murdoch?" PBS *Frontline* video.

13 Bower, Tom, *Maxwell the Outsider*, Aurum Press, London, 1988.

14 Despite this global reach, News Corp has—quite legally—mastered the art of minimizing its tax liabilities. One calculation estimated that News Corp, the umbrella corporation, paid a meager 1.2 percent on profits between 1985 and 1995.

15 News Corporation, 1997 Annual Report.

16 Murdoch, Rupert, "The century of networking."

17 Mintzberg, Henry, *The Nature of Managerial Work*, McGraw Hill, New York, 1973.

1

Go with the Flow

You got to be careful if you don't know where you're going, because you might not get there.

YOGI BERRA

DON'T BELIEVE IN ANYTHING

Contrary to what you might read—or like to believe—the great businesspeople usually don't believe in anything. They are corporate atheists. Their faith is the dollar or the ego. If you want proof read the autobiographies of successful businessmen and women. They are extended ego trips usually dominated by avarice and self-justification—or both. Rupert Murdoch is no exception. He is a highly driven and hugely successful businessman. His creed is business. Outside business there appears little else. He has a yacht and houses around the world, but he does not spend money on art or fast cars or wine cellars. Apart from business, he appears an empty vessel—to the outside world at least. "For all the fuss that he has aroused in four decades of wheeling and dealing, Murdoch remains an inscrutable figure—an apostle of global communica-

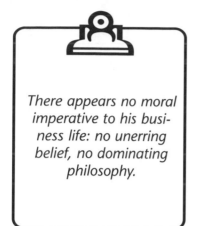

There appears no moral imperative to his business life: no unerring belief, no dominating philosophy.

tions who is a master of not telling the world what he really thinks," noted a *BusinessWeek* article.[1]

Murdoch has talked of having a moral compass to all his activities. However, if there is morality it is difficult to find. His father's family was religious, but Rupert Murdoch is presumably comfortable with the topless models in his newspapers and the intrusions into people's privacy. There appears no moral imperative to his business life: no unerring belief, no dominating philosophy. This is partly because his interests and activities are so immense and diverse, but what drives Murdoch has always been difficult to pinpoint. It shifts with the times.

Look, for example, at Murdoch's political affiliations. From reading newspaper and magazine profiles, you would quickly conclude that Rupert Murdoch is rabidly right wing. That's the media image.

It is not without foundation. At times Murdoch has appeared to be solidly right wing. In November 1996, he gave $1 million to the California Republican Party. He was one of Prime Minister Margaret Thatcher's staunchest supporters. Prior to her electoral triumph in 1979 and in the years that followed, Mrs. Thatcher received steadfast support from Murdoch. She was reputedly fond of popping into the editorial offices of the Murdoch-owned *Sun* newspaper to receive wisdom and whisky. Murdoch's speeches could always be relied upon to include talk about the power and righteousness of market forces. Murdoch and

Thatcher sang very loudly from the same song book and they sang even louder after Murdoch's battles with the unions at Wapping.

The mistake is to believe that Murdoch would allow any political beliefs to affect business decisions. He has shifted with the times. In the 1980s he was in tune with the political ambitions and agenda of the right. He seemed to be on their side. But to him, backing Thatcher or Tony Blair in the U.K., Gough Whitlam or Malcolm Fraser in Australia, does not appear to be a matter of conscience or belief. He is the ultimate pragmatist who recognizes that it is better to back winners than losers. "His political alliances have nothing to do with ideology," noted one newspaper.

When it comes to picking political parties, Rupert Murdoch is brilliantly—almost outrageously—pragmatic. Politicians have short memories and are always willing to listen to someone with such influence and deep pockets. This is just as well. Superficial scrutiny of Murdoch's political affiliations reveals a steady stream of impossible U-turns—well, U-turns if you were actually a believer in the first place.

In 1972 he supported the Australian Labour Party's Gough Whitlam as Prime Minister. In 1975 Murdoch supported the Conservative Malcolm Fraser and engaged in a newspaper campaign against Whitlam described by one witness as "the most extraordinarily ruthless and one-sided political coverage I think any of us can remember."[2]

Murdoch goes with the flow in the hope that he can make it work for him. Early in 1998, there was yet another flurry of media coverage of Murdoch. Its central theme was that British Prime Minister Tony Blair was too close to Murdoch and that he was directly sup-

Murdoch on Gorbachev:

"The man's still a communist."

porting Murdoch's business aspirations. It was suggested that Blair had sought to persuade the Italian Prime Minister to help a Murdoch deal in Italy. (It was one Murdoch deal—with Silvio Berlusconi's television company, Mediaset—that did not happen.)

What was amazing about this entire scenario was that there was little or no mention of the fact that Murdoch had been a stalwart supporter of Margaret Thatcher. Yet less than 20 years after throwing his weight behind Mrs. Thatcher, Murdoch is apparently so friendly with a Labour Party prime minister that it is a matter of concern.

To complicate matters a little further, during his youth Murdoch was generally regarded as being left leaning when it came to politics. At Oxford, a bust of Lenin adorned Murdoch's mantelpiece. Murdoch reportedly annoyed his father by referring to Lenin as "the great teacher." This had been long forgotten when, three decades later, Murdoch was strongly skeptical of Mikhail Gorbachev's overtures to the West in the 1980s. He was not happy with the *Sunday Times'* serialization of Gorbachev's book (published by another of his companies). "The man's still a Communist," he complained to then editor Andrew Neil.[3]

Murdoch knows the value of the printed word. One of Murdoch's techniques is to commission glowing books about or by politicians. (Robert Maxwell pursued a similar policy to ingratiate himself with East European Communist leaders.) Murdoch companies have signed major book contracts for politicians including Mikhail Gorbachev, Margaret Thatcher, Deng Xiaoping's daughter (Deng himself was too old and feeble to write a book—though not apparently to run a country) and Newt Gingrich (for a whopping $4.5 million). It would be difficult to come up with a more bizarre list of political bedfellows. These contracts are not simply about book publishing. Deng had a very interesting life and ran the biggest country in the world, but his was not the story publishers were falling over themselves to sign. The book of the life of Deng was not worth the reported $1 million advance. It was a loss leader. The *Columbia Journalism Review* called it "a fawning—and historically flawed and commercially non-viable—portrait."[4] The question must always be, a loss leader for what?

It is not surprising that the link between the politicians is that, at the time Rupert Murdoch took an interest in their careers, they were on the verge of power or already in power. Murdoch has a habit of backing winners. Losers do not figure on his radar. In the 1977 mayoral campaign in New York his *New York Post* endorsed Ed Koch rather than Mario Cuomo. Explaining this selection, Murdoch reputedly said: "It's very simple. There are two and a half million Jews in New York and one million Italians."[5] You can't get any more pragmatic than that.

Murdoch tends to get his bets in early. Before the Labour Party won its stunning 1997 U.K. election victory, Murdoch had already established himself as their ally. Tony Blair was invited to address a gathering of News International executives. Then Murdoch's *Sun* newspaper publicly came out for Blair early in the election campaign. This dealt a body blow to the

Conservative Party—as Murdoch knew it would. News Corp's 1997 Annual Report made it clear that it fully realized the import of the *Sun's* decision: "In an election year, the paper's most notable success was in the political arena; its judgement in backing new Labour leader Tony Blair was shared by the electorate which gave him a significant majority." Since then the *Sun* has occasionally flexed its muscles with a voice of dissent just to ensure the government knows who really pulls the strings.

None of this means that Rupert Murdoch is a card-carrying member of the Labour Party or, indeed, of the Conservative Party. If there are any cards, he is holding them tightly to his chest. Like anyone in business, Murdoch has sought to influence events in his favor. Murdoch's machinations are a little more ostentatious than some. But they are ostentatious because of who he is rather than what he is doing.

Strip away the political power games and the big-name politicians, and Murdoch is simply a fantastic networker. For an apparently isolated, highly driven individual, he spends a great deal of time making sure that he is well-connected. His connections embrace people you would not normally expect them to embrace. Evangelist Pat Robertson, for example, called for a boycott of advertisers on Fox's sitcom, *Married ... with Children*. The ultra-right-wing Robertson did not approve of the content. Murdoch clearly did not bear a grudge and has done business with Robertson since. Robertson's current view of the offending sitcom would be interesting.

Elsewhere, Murdoch is continually exercising his networking antennae. In the fall of 1997, Murdoch joined the board of directors of the influen-

GO WITH THE FLOW

- *Move with the times—if your finger is on yesterday's pulse, you are dead. Murdoch sniffs out where the power is moving and boards the bandwagon. He does so not with a loud yahoo and proclamation of conversion, but quietly.*

- *Ideas develop and evolve—so, too, must yours. The right wing agenda of the 1980s was readily embraced by Murdoch, but his beliefs have evolved.*

- *Do not overcommit to one cause—today's cause celebre is tomorrow's has-been. There is a difficult balance to be struck. Murdoch embraces and supports causes, but manages not to be inextricably linked to them in a way that might later prove damaging.*

- *Constantly update and develop your network of contacts. If your network is out of date (or out of power), you are out of date and out of favor. Networking is a daily commitment, not a monthly social. Success requires that executives must become more efficient users of their networks. Networking is the cornerstone of good career management. KPMG Career Consulting encourages managers to make a basic list of their networks. Managers are expected to come up with over 100 names.*

- *Get close to the corridors of power. For better or worse, politicians change things. Their decisions affect businesses. If it is possible to become involved in the decision-making process, do so.*

- *But don't become a politician. Leave politics to the politicians but ensure that they leave your business to you.*

- *Put your faith in the next deal rather than some big idea or philosophy. Overbearing philosophies are more likely to be straitjackets than routes to bigger profits.*

tial right-wing think tank, the Cato Institute. On the board, Murdoch rubs shoulders with TCI chief John Malone, among others. Murdoch is making connections continually and placing bets on where power is heading and where the deals can be made. His hunches have generally been proved reliable.

NOTES

1 Landler, Mark, "Rupert the inscrutable," *BusinessWeek,* August 2, 1993.
2 MacCullum, Mungo, *Who's Afraid of Rupert Murdoch?* PBS Video.
3 Neil, Andrew, "Rupert the fear," *The Guardian,* March 2, 1998.
4 Baker, Russ, "Murdoch's mean machine," *Columbia Journalism Review*, May/June 1998.
5 Shawcross, William, *Murdoch,* Chatto & Windus, London, 1992.

Goodbye, Mr. Nice Guy

*To subdue the enemy's forces without fighting is
the summit of skill. The best approach is to attack
the other side's strategy; next best is to attack his
alliances; next best is to attack his soldiers; the
worst is to attack cities."*

SUN TZU

PERFORMANCE OR SIBERIA

According to the commentators and theorists, this is the age of empowerment. The era of corporate dictatorship is past. Spiritual awareness and self-knowledge are in. Nice guys rule. Of course, as Rupert Murdoch would be the first to tell you, theory and reality are often poles apart. In the boardrooms of the world, reality remains much the same as it ever was. Empower all you like, but it is a ruthless world.

This is repeatedly confirmed by the regular stream of reports, articles and books on the skills you need to reach the top. Despite what theorists would have us believe, the old skills are still the ones that help forge brilliant careers. Typically, a study by two Henley Management College academics provided hard evidence based on tracking the careers of 72 managers over seven years. The more successful managers in the study displayed a willingness to take risks, were more

"Trust is not earned by being a nice guy."

HAROLD GENEEN

decisive and forceful, and showed more energy and initiative than their less successful counterparts. The resulting profile of a high-flier did not include many of the currently fashionable ideas such as learning and empowering others. Indeed, the high-fliers were good at controlling and adept at planning and organizing. They were, if the business gurus are to be believed, a throwback to another era. Out of vogue these competencies may be, but research suggests that they continue to play a key role in the careers of successful executives, executives like Rupert Murdoch.[1]

Murdoch is from the old school. "Trust is not earned by being a nice guy. It comes with character and competence. I say you must be a person of character, one willing to be responsible for people—their lives and their hopes," wrote former ITT chief Harold Geneen in one of his final articles.[2] Business is not about being nice—and a lot of thoroughly nice people act in a ruthless fashion at work. Allied to pragmatism is Murdoch's undoubted ruthlessness.

After all, the populist bent of his tabloid newspapers is built on a form of moral ruthlessness. "He's a complex personality, because if you read the editorials in his newspapers they are very highly moralistic and they are very highly principled and so on, and yet they appear in papers that are almost without principles journalistically," said Thomas Kiernan, one of many who have written books about Murdoch. The product is more important than a few scruples.

Murdochian morality is similar to his political thinking. It is easy to believe in the free market if you are hugely successful within it, less so if you are excluded from it. It is easy to make moral judgements if your own private life is stable, less so when it falls apart. "Against the background of his own impeccable family life, Murdoch has felt able to intrude upon, mock and often break up less successful marriages, insisting all the way that it was not his own behavior, but the flings and indiscretions of the subjects of these stories that were at fault," concluded one newspaper article.[3]

Similarly, if the business situation requires that someone be sacked or sent to corporate Siberia, Murdoch displays little hesitation. He decides and they depart. And if Murdoch can drive out the competition, he will try his damnedest to do so.

MANAGING PEOPLE

Aside from the ruthless application of the moral high ground, Murdoch is ruthless in his management of people. This appears a damning indictment. In reality it is not. Show me a CEO who is not, on occasion, prepared to be ruthless and I will show you a failed CEO. No matter who you are, ruthlessness is a necessary part of the top job.

While News Corp is an exciting, fast-moving company to work for, no one ever suggested that working for Rupert Murdoch was easy. It is anything but.

The image of Rupert Murdoch is of some fear-inducing ogre who motivates simply by fear. Undoubtedly, Murdoch motivates partly by fear. An article by ex-Murdoch employee Andrew Neil on Murdoch's motivational style was entitled "Rupert the fear." "For courtiers to survive at the Court of King Rupert, they have to be adept at anticipating their master's wishes and acting in his interests," says Neil. Courtiers no doubt do much the same if they work for Andrew Neil or anyone else. Inevitably, this is only part of the story.

The reality is that Murdoch manages people with much the same ruthlessness as he manages other parts of his business empire. There is no middle ground. People perform or they are dispatched. Performance or Siberia. Andrew Neil, the former *Sunday Times* editor, attributes this partly to Murdoch's austere Scottish Presbyterian background. "It makes him reserved about spending too much on the baubles of billionaires. He has beautiful houses on three continents, but he actually lives quite modestly, eating simply and drinking moderately, even preferring taxis to limousines," noted Neil in his autobiography. "He travels alone, but then he is a loner. It took him ages to acquire his own executive jet, despite his endless globetrotting." Murdoch guards his wealth, his family and his feelings. "The only people who are really close to him are his wife, his children, his sister, Helen, and his mother. He has no real friends. He does not allow himself to become intimate with anybody else, for he never knows when he will have to turn on them," says Neil, who has reason to know as he was one of those Murdoch eventually turned against.

Yet the fallout from aggrieved former members of staff appears minimal. "His tolerance of mistakes is very limited. Mr. Murdoch has fired over 40 publishers and editors, including one of his father's best friends, and Clay Felker, one of America's most successful editors," noted another article. "Because anger or jealousy do not seem to be the cause of these dismissals, employee morale does not seem to suffer. Mr. Murdoch is able to convince those around him that the people he fired are still great, but are not right for the moment."[4]

BEATING THE COMPETITION

"A Prince ought to have no other aim or thought, nor select anything else for his study, than war and its rules and discipline; for this is the sole art that belongs to him who rules," advised Machiavelli.

When it comes to competition, Rupert Murdoch does not take prisoners. Business is war. Indeed, Murdoch has cheerfully described life as "a series of interlocking wars."[5]

If Murdoch generates fear within his own employees, he scares competitors with a unique brand of bluster and unadulterated power. "Competition generates energy, rewards winners and punishes losers. It is therefore the fuel for the economy," says management guru Charles Handy. Rupert Murdoch is a ruthless competitor with no interest in being a loser. "Someone can beat you up or run you over, but if you don't give them a few bruises in return, they can do it to the next person who comes along," he says. "It would be very

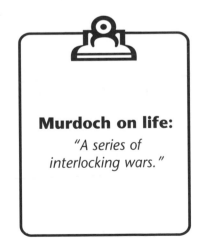

Murdoch on life:
"A series of interlocking wars."

Murdoch on competition:

"in every area of economic activity in which competition is attainable, it is much to be preferred to monopoly."

bad for News Corporation for people to think that we were a patsy that can be run over and disenfranchised."[6]

He has no time for fancy strategizing. Murdoch competes to win. The trouble is that winning means wiping out the competition. This leads to the vexing question of monopolies. Given his media domination, Murdoch has actually fared very well in avoiding trouble with monopoly regulations. His carefully arranged networks of influence obviously play a part in this. In 1997 News Corp newspapers in the U.K. accounted for 35 percent of circulation market share on weekdays and 39 percent on Sundays. This was nearly double the closest competitor.[7] "I start from a simple principle: In every area of economic activity in which competition is attainable, it is much to be preferred to monopoly," says Murdoch.[8] But if you compete aggressively and are successful, a monopoly is inevitable.

Monopolies or not, Murdoch's career has been marked by a willingness to confront competition head on. It is not subtle, but it works. Look at the clash with the unions at Wapping. Don Ohlmeyer of NBC has said: "People genuinely fear him, and that's a good position to be in in this business."[9]

In October 1996 Murdoch told shareholders at the News Corp annual meeting: "We intend to . . . use sports as a battering ram and a lead offering in all our pay-television operations." How many other CEOs do you hear talking of entering new markets in such blithely brutal terms? Or in terms that are so simple?

The downside of Murdoch's style is that decisiveness and ruthlessness are sledgehammers, and more subtle tools are sometimes required. In pursuit of competitive advantage, Murdoch occasionally drives straight on, trampling on some folks' sensibilities.

Murdoch was once again in the news in early 1998 when there was a furor over the prospect of HarperCollins, a News International company, publishing a book by former Hong Kong Governor Chris Patten about his time overseeing the handover of Hong Kong to China. It was anticipated that the book, *East and West,* would be hostile to the Chinese regime. Given that Patten had spent five years being hostile to the Chinese, this was hardly a surprise. But Murdoch has ambitions for China and was not happy about the prospect of an arm of his company upsetting the Chinese. His reaction, according to the newspapers, was to instruct his executives to "Kill the [f-ing] book!" The executives jumped.

They also jumped into a public relations mire. The U.K. chief of HarperCollins, Eddie Bell, chose his words carefully after the bombs had been dropped. "KRM has outlined to me the negative aspects of publication," he said with what he may have thought was diplomatic brilliance.[10] It did not help. HarperCollins' highly respected editor in chief Stuart Proffitt resigned, outraged authors wrote letters to newspapers and all the papers not owned by Murdoch covered every word in huge, gleeful detail. Murdoch's papers tiptoed around the subject with all the nimbleness of elephants in a minefield. Pictures of Murdoch in jovial mood with the Chinese president Jiang Zemin did not help. "Murdoch's decision to axe Patten's book may have cheered a few bureaucrats in Beijing, but it gravely damaged his reputation in countries where he makes his real money," concluded one newspaper.[11]

The only beneficiary of this storm was Chris Patten. His contract with HarperCollins was canceled so he departed to a new publisher with an advance (reportedly of $200,000) in his pocket and a mountain of publicity. All he had to do was write the book.

Where does a debacle like the Patten affair leave Rupert Murdoch? With egg on his face, perhaps, but largely unaffected. He looked bad for a few days, but in the end his long-term aspirations were deemed more important than quibbles about editorial independence.

GOODBYE, MR. NICE GUY

♦ *Manage people as rigorously as other corporate assets. To do otherwise is to do them and the business a disservice. If someone is not doing the job - for whatever reason—they should not be in it.*

♦ *Recruit strong people. One of the commonest traits in recruitment is to recruit people in your own image. It is notable that Murdoch's most successful executives have themselves tended to be larger-than-life personalities. At* The Sun *the first editor was Larry Lamb. Then came Kelvin MacKenzie. At the* Sunday Times, *Murdoch developed the career of Andrew Neil, a robustly right-wing Scotsman with an opinion on everything. At Sky there was Sam Chisholm. Look also at the politicians Murdoch has been most closely identified with. First was Margaret Thatcher, a strong woman with a single-minded vision of what she wanted to achieve. Then came Tony Blair, a leader who*

---

managed to transform an organization (the Labour Party) and provide a credible vision for the future of the country. Murdoch is not afraid of strong people if they help the company achieve its objectives.

♦ *Backtracking is weakness.* Murdoch believes that in a world of bluster, you have to be prepared to stand firm. Sticking by decisions—even if they prove to be wrong—is the only way.

♦ *Compete to win.* Markets—and competitors—have a nasty habit of snapping back. Dominate them. Murdoch does not want to be second in a market, he wants to lead it. The result is that the competition is fearful of his next move, even if it is quite innocuous. "Mr Murdoch . . . keeps a low profile, but his backstage machinations have struck fear in the hearts of media overlords everywhere," said the magazine Red Herring.[12]

♦ *Accept short-term criticism for long-term gain.* The Patten episode was a fiasco of Murdoch's own making, but there was no chance of him backtracking. The pain was deemed to be worth the potential long-term gain.

NOTES

1   Dulewicz, Victor and Herbert, Peter, "General management competences and personality," Henley Research Centre Working Paper, 1996.

2   Geneen, Harold, "Inspire confidence and trust," *Management General*, 1997.

3   Milliken, Robert and Cornwell, Tim, "Never the little woman," *Independent on Sunday*, April 26, 1998.

4   "The saucy Aussie," *Red Herring*, April 1995.

5   Farhi, Paul, "Murdoch, all business," *Washington Post*, February 12, 1995.

6 *Independent on Sunday*, February 15, 1998.

7 News Corporation, Annual Report, 1997.

8 Solomon, Norman, "Media moguls on board," *Think Tank Monitor*, January/February 1998.

9 Baker, Russ, "Murdoch's mean machine," *Columbia Journalism Review*, May/June 1998.

10 Baker, Russ, "Murdoch's mean machine."

11 Higgins, Andrew, "Long view leaves businessmen short," *The Guardian*, April 18, 1998.

12 Gove, Alex, "Lord of the skies," *Red Herring*, Issue 44, July 1997.

Place Your Bets

Take calculated risks. That is quite different from being rash.

GENERAL GEORGE S. PATTON

BALANCING INTUITION WITH ANALYSIS

In China gambling is illegal. Yet every Thursday evening and Sunday afternoon, massive crowds watch and bet on horse racing courtesy of the Guangzhou Jockey Club. They are not gambling. Instead, they are participating in a "horse-racing intelligence competition."[1]

Rupert Murdoch takes risks. Big risks. He backs hunches. He is a gambler. "He took a huge gamble. He made the investment before any of the questions were answered. That sort of uncertainty is inimical to good investing," criticized one investment analyst.

While at school, Murdoch sold horse manure and trapped

Murdoch's financial brinkmanship is legendary and continuous. He is juggling a lot of balls.

rabbits for their skins. He then gambled the money. While at Geelong Grammar School, Murdoch would cycle to Melbourne to go to the races at Flemington Race Course. While at Oxford, he nipped over the Channel to Deauville in France to invest his money at the casino. He enjoys the thrill of gambling, of playing for big stakes. He has bet on newspapers, on TV, and on distant satellites. It is a high-stakes intelligence competition.

In 1990 Murdoch nearly went bust, with borrowings of over $7 billion. "There was a notable difference, it was said, between Maxwell and Murdoch. The Australian owed the banks so much that banks could not afford to allow him to go broke without bankrupting themselves. Maxwell's business was too small for his and his bank's survival to be dependent upon each other," noted Tom Bower in his biography of Maxwell.[2] Murdoch's financial brinkmanship is legendary and continuous. He is juggling a lot of balls. "Some people feel there are too many things being chased. When is enough enough?" one analyst recently asked. But Murdoch carries on launching one ball after another in the air—and catching most of them successfully.

When it comes off, it looks fantastic. At the end of 1990 Murdoch merged his U.K. satellite TV company Sky with its competitor to form BSkyB. Sky had helped push Murdoch to the precipice. At the time, it had $2.7 billion worth of debt. It was one of the biggest bets of his career—or of any other career. In 1994, the new company, BSkyB, announced profits of $280 million and has been paying back Murdoch's investment ever since. Big stakes bring big wins.

After saving the company in 1990 one would have expected Murdoch to lower the stakes for a while, to back off. But what would a true gambler do? He would do what Murdoch did—he upped the ante by seeking to create a truly global satellite broadcasting network. This is a true gambler at work.

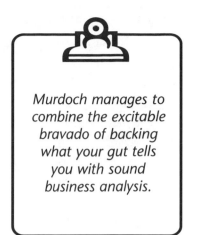

Murdoch manages to combine the excitable bravado of backing what your gut tells you with sound business analysis.

What is interesting about Murdoch's approach to risk is that it manages to combine the excitable bravado of backing what your gut tells you with sound business analysis. Regular, detailed financial reporting has long been a key feature of News Corp's style. In the early 1960s, Murdoch brought in Mervyn Rich to beat his financial systems into shape. One of Rich's innovations was a weekly financial reporting system. This ensured that Murdoch had the freshest facts available on the performance of every business every single week. Problems could be identified early on and, most importantly, acted upon.

The trouble is that while business analysis can be taught—business schools teach little else—the mysteries of intuition remain buried deep inside the individual. As Rupert Murdoch has proved, intuition is a powerful—but dangerous—decision-making weapon. When he was pouring money into Sky TV in the early 1990s, Murdoch was not following analytical advice. All the commentators and analysts with the figures at their disposal were shaking their heads with bewilderment. Murdoch carried on pouring money into what was the commercial equivalent of a black hole.

Murdoch may be a stubborn man, but he is also willing to follow what he thinks, or knows, to be right.

If a particular route is the right one for the business, he will follow it to the very end. But how does this relate to mere mortals?

"At any given moment one is conscious of only a small section of what one knows. Intuition allows one to draw on that vast storehouse of unconscious knowledge that includes not only everything that one has experienced or learned either consciously or subliminally, but also the infinite reservoir of the collection or universal consciousness, in which individual separateness and ego boundaries are transcended," says the psychologist Francis E. Vaughan. Intuition, if Vaughan is to be believed, gives you access to the collective wisdom of civilization—something no software package can so far achieve.

Herein lies the first problem with intuition. It is all-embracing and, as a result, steeped in vagueness. It is inexplicable, but can explain all. It is a human constant, but capable of disappearing into the ether. "It is fashionable stupidity to regard everything one cannot explain as fraud," noted Carl Jung. "The term [intuition] does not denote something contrary to reason, but something outside the province of reason." Jung, of course, never had to explain that to a roomful of News Corp stockholders and investment analysts.

When managers are quizzed about what intuition actually is, they offer a wide range of answers. Research into intuition by Jagdish Parikh of IMD in Switzerland found that when 1312 top and senior managers from nine countries were asked, "What is intuition?" they replied in a variety of ways. (What is equally interesting is that each of these responses is credible and plausible. If a manager wishes to view intuition as instinct, you can't really argue.)

Research carried out by the British academic Phil Hodgson,[3] *What Do High Performance Managers Really Do?*, suggests that managers who use their intuition effectively and continuously are likely to have a number of clear characteristics:

♦ They make decisions quickly and confidently. They are willing to back their judgement and don't spend large periods of time weighing things up.

♦ They use data only when necessary. Not for them the computer printout containing every single statistic available.

♦ They recognize intuition as a skill, part of their managerial armory.

♦ They accept and encourage ideas, whatever their source or apparent usefulness, at every stage.

♦ They act on intuitive judgements, rather than questioning them.

♦ They accept no rigid or wrong method of doing things. If something feels, looks or seems right, they will do it.

Murdoch is not alone in utilizing intuition effectively. Interviews with some of the business world's greatest names quickly reveal steadfast usage of intuition. "You don't have to discuss things. You can sense it. The tingle is as important as the intellect," argued Sir David Simon, then chairman of British Petroleum.[4] On his decision not to elevate Jeffrey Katzenberg to

"You don't have to discuss things. You can sense it. The tingle is as important as the intellect."

president, Disney chief Michael Eisner said it was down to "a lot of very logical reasons and also some intuitional reasons." "Once I have a feeling for the choices, I have no problems with the decisions," says IBM chief Lou Gerstner.[5] Or take this description of Eisner by Barry Diller, formerly Eisner's boss at ABC and Paramount (and later at Murdoch's Fox): "Michael looks like Goofy, and he often acts like Goofy, and he's definitely in the body of Goofy! But he's got one of the most smartly spirited minds that I've ever come across. You can see the electrical charges moving from one point to another in his brain. Spectacular instincts. Of course, he's not

WHAT IS INTUITION?

Description	%
Decision/perception without recourse to logical/rational methods	23.4
Inherent perception; inexplicable comprehension; a feeling that comes from within	17.1
Integration of previous experience; processing of accumulated information	16.8
Gut feeling	12.0
Decision/solution to problem, without complete data/facts	8.6
Sixth Sense	7.4
Spontaneous perception/vision	7.3
Insight	6.7
Subconscious process	6.1
Instinct	5.7

always right, and when it comes to that he has a somewhat tractionless memory."[6] If you are Rupert Murdoch, such "spectacular instincts" are worth hundreds of millions of dollars.

Virgin boss Richard Branson is another corporate leader who seems willing and able to follow his instinct for an opportunity. Branson recalls his decision to go into the airline business in 1984: "It was a move which in pure economic terms everybody thought was mad, including my closest friends, but it was something which I felt we could bring something to that others were not bringing."[7] It didn't add up, but Branson thought there was something there and persisted.

General Electric's Jack Welch is another who has pronounced himself as intuitive—or, at least, in touch with his senses. "Here at head office, we don't go very deep into much of anything, but we have a smell of everything," says Welch. "Our job is capital allocation— intellectual and financial. Smell, feel, touch, listen, then allocate. Make bets, with people and dollars. And make mistakes."[8]

In reality, Rupert Murdoch does not rely purely on intuition. Sometimes the intuitive component is exaggerated. Like other top managers of major corporations, he lives in an atmosphere of analysis, constantly fed both quantitative and qualitative analyses by an army of highly skilled professionals. Indeed, with today's complex pay packages involving deferred compensation, performance-based bonuses and stock options, it takes a certain level of analytical sophistication for any CEO just to understand what she or he is getting paid. For many of those instinctively intuitive managers who genuinely lack or decline to rely on their own analytical skills, working closely with more analytical colleagues offers a counterweight. (Branson, for example, is counseled by Virgin's finance director in the same way Lord Hanson once counseled his colorful partner, Lord White.)

"Intuition is not a process that operates independently of analysis," argues Herbert Simon. "It is a fallacy to contrast 'analytic' and 'intuitive' styles of management. Intuition and judgment—at least good judgment—are simply analyses frozen into habit and into the capacity for rapid response through recognition."[9]

Combining reliable intuition with sound information and analysis is a potent commercial cocktail.

Intuition is fast

As intuition comes from within, no time is wasted in referring the problem to others or involving others. With no burdensome hierarchy, News Corp moves fast.

Intuition is creative

Beyond any doubt most truly creative solutions involve an intuitive leap at some point. Every one of us has at some time had the answer to a thorny problem pop up while in the shower. There has always been a recognition that intuition, properly harnessed, can produce solutions far beyond the routine. However, relying on intuition does not automatically produce valuable creative ideas. Just because all creativity requires intuition does not mean all intuition produces creativity. For this reason many have tried to develop a dependable system to translate intuition into creativity, to systematize intuition. Brainstorming, which became popular in the 1980s, is the most common routinized "creative" exercise managers involve themselves in. There are also other techniques to capture intuitive, creative solutions—mind mapping, Delphi Technique, etc. All of these techniques suffer from a common problem: It is easy enough to conjure up intuition on demand. It is far harder to generate *creative intuition* on demand. Murdoch and News Corp have shown a consistent ability to think outside the box, to think creatively to uncover new solutions and new markets.

Intuition is fun

You can't overlook the fact that intuition is relatively easy. There is no need for lengthy hours of number crunching. There is no need for time-consuming case studies. It can be fun.

Intuition is exciting

Like tightrope walking, intuition is precarious and addictive. "One of the things that is confusing and almost intoxicating when you are growing a business is that you really have little way of determining what the problems are," observes Michael Dell.[10] In many cases, even in well-developed businesses, you have even fewer ways of determining what the perfect answer is. There is always a temptation to say "Ready, Fire, Aim." That lack of a safety net can be exhilarating.

Intuition is personal

Intuition, of course, has one great allure: It cannot be turned into a management theory. To practicing managers this is often persuasive, or at least feels persuasive. It is their own, highly individualistic slant on management. Of course, there are continuing attempts to bring intuition into the mainstream, but it remains highly individualistic. Most of us pride ourselves, at least to some extent, on our gut. Take it or leave it, it is ours alone. Emulate Rupert Murdoch's use of intuition at your own risk.

The downside to using intuition is equally simple.

Intuition is completely personal and subjective

Intuition makes every discussion personal. If I tell you that my gut tells me something, your only response is to say that my gut is right (end of debate) or wrong (beginning of personal animosity). It is therefore hard to choose between two different answers produced by intuition. Murdoch's domination of News Corp means that there is not usually a choice.

People don't trust intuitive answers

Leadership theorists Phil Hodgson and Randall White asked many executives whether they used "inner sense" (their word for intuition). More than 80 percent said they did, but fewer than 30 percent said they would admit it in the boardroom. It is simply not persuasive or credible to attribute an important decision to a "feeling." There needs to be a great deal more if an argument is to be persuasive.

Intuition is not replicable or testable

You cannot rely on intuition to be there when you need it, and certainly not to be right or even accurate when you need it to be. "Analysis, when done correctly with the right kind of data, gives answers that are precisely correct," notes Henry Mintzberg. "Intuition, in contrast, when applied to problems with which it can deal, tends to be only approximately correct ('in the ballpark' being the popular American expression)."[11]

Intuition can intensify debates rather than resolving them

The senior person tends to win in an intuition-led debate. As such intuition is highly undemocratic. If the CEO's intuition says that it is a good idea, you need a better rejoinder than saying that your intuition disagrees.

Intuition emphasizes action rather than thinking

In their excellent book, Frederick Hilmer and Lex Donaldson[12] argue that the belief that management is about "doing, walking about, making decisions on the spot" has led to a belief that management is action and action is based on intuition. Hilmer and Donaldson argue that this tends to undermine the intellectual content of the work of management and hence the need for management education as well as the need for analysis and reflection, the thoughtful side of management. "Don't just do something. Stand there," advocates MIT's Jay Forrester.

As Hilmer and Donaldson observe, managers focus on actions because, faced with the day-to-day demands of running a business, they cannot afford to constantly renew their understanding. Murdoch would argue that doing something is always better than being stationary.

WHEN TO LEAVE IT TO INTUITION

Sam Hill of Helios Consulting and coauthor of Radical Marketing *provides five problems best solved by intuition:*

1   *Very personal decisions, such as who to marry— although some might well argue that a little more analysis would reduce the divorce rate.*

2   *Problems for which the costs of a wrong decision are very low, such as where to have lunch.*

3   *Questions about which there is no available data. (However, you need to be careful. There is almost always more data than you think.)*

4   *Problems for which the data that does exist is very suspect. All data are not created equal. Ask the developers of Frost 90, a clear bourbon, who were convinced by market research that the declining popularity of bourbon and simultaneous rise of vodka was the result of color preferences. What people say they want is not always what they do want.*

5   *Questions far out in the future. Analysis is great for many things, but it is not very good at predicting the future. "Forecasting is very hard, especially about the future," quipped Niels Bohr. Every year leading organizations and newspapers compile predictions of economists on GDP, inflation, etc. All of these economists use ultra-sophisticated analytical models, yet the results vary widely.*

PLACE YOUR BETS

- *Risk taking is the essence of managerial decision making. If you don't enjoy risk, you won't enjoy management. Rupert Murdoch patently enjoys the thrill of risk. During the frenzy of excitement surrounding News Corp's potential collapse in 1990, Murdoch was reputedly more fretful than normal because he missed the day-to-day adrenaline of deal making. Saving a company does not appeal to him as much as building one.*

- *Respect intuition, but feed in the figures. Decisions made solely on intuition are the riskiest possible. Murdoch may trust his intuition, but he also ensures that he receives the latest figures from each and every one of his business units. He is in touch.*

- *Keep your nerve when the race is on. When your horse starts going backwards, you might wish you had never placed the bet. Gamblers think otherwise. As one bet fails, they are seeking out a new stake, a new sure thing. Losing is part of the game. It is no thrill, but gamblers know that you have to lose to win. Real winners lose and resolve never to make the same mistake again.*

NOTES

1 "China's uncertain odds," *The Economist*, September 2, 1995.

2 Bower, Tom, *Maxwell the Outsider*, Aurum Press, London, 1988.

3 Hodgson, Phil and Crainer, Stuart, *What Do High Performance Managers Really Do?*, Trans-Atlantic Publications, Incorporated, 1993.

4 Quoted in Hosking, P., "The leader's leader," *Independent on Sunday*, December 31, 1995.

5 Quoted in Cornwell, R., "The iconoclast at IBM," *Independent on Sunday*, August 1, 1993.

6 Quoted in Huey, J., "Eisner explains everything," *Fortune*, April 17, 1995.

7 de Vries, M. Kets and Dick, R., *Branson's Virgin: The Coming of Age of a Counter-Cultural Enterprise*, INSEAD, Fontainebleau, 1995.

8 Quoted in Jackson, T. and Gowers, A., "Big enough to make mistakes," *Financial Times*, December 21, 1995.

9 Simon, Herbert, "Making management decisions: the role of intuition and emotion," *Academy of Management Executives*, February 1, 1987, pp. 57–64.

10 Quoted in Jacob, R., "The resurrection of Michael Dell," *Fortune*, September 18, 1995.

11 Mintzberg, Henry, *The Rise and Fall of Strategic Planning*, Prentice Hall, Englewood Cliffs, NJ, 1994, p. 327.

12 Hilmer, Frederick and Donaldson, Lex, *Management Redeemed: Debunking the Fads That Undermine Our Corporations*, Simon & Schuster Trade, New York, 1996

Lead from the Front

Leadership produces change. That is its primary function.

JOHN KOTTER, HARVARD BUSINESS SCHOOL

MURDOCH THE LEADER

Rupert Murdoch leads from the front. Period. The nature of leadership is something that has been discussed and dissected ad infinitum by business school academics, amateur psychologists and anyone with access to the complete works of Napoleon and a pen. Not surprisingly, opinions differ. There are reputed to be 400 different definitions of the word *leadership*.

One of the best-known leadership theorists is Warren Bennis, who has acted as an adviser to four U.S. Presidents. Bennis argues that leadership is not a rare skill; leaders are made rather than born; leaders are usually ordinary people—or apparently ordinary—rather than charismatic; leadership is not solely the preserve of those at the top of the organization—it is relevant at all levels; finally, leadership is not about control, direction or manipulation.

Bennis' best-known leadership research involved 90 of America's leaders.[1] These included Neil Armstrong, the coach of the LA Rams, orchestral conductors, and businesspeople such as Ray Kroc of McDonald's. From the 90 leaders, four common abilities were identified: management of attention, of meaning, of trust and of self. It is interesting to see how Rupert Murdoch matches up against this leadership template.

VISION

Management of attention is, according to Bennis, a question of vision. Bennis defines leadership as: "The capacity to create a compelling vision and translate it into action and sustain it." Successful leaders have a vision that other people believe in and treat as their own.

Vision has been a notable facet of Murdoch's management style throughout his career. He has looked to the future and, with sometimes startling persistence, hung onto his belief in what the future would bring. His perseverance with Sky Television company in the U.K. is just one example of Murdoch's willingness to stick with his vision.

Of course, having a vision is one thing; converting it into successful action is another. But if you have the belief and persistence, Murdoch has proved that you can make it happen. So on Bennis' first leadership trait, Murdoch scores high.

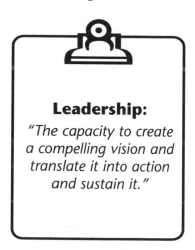

Leadership:

"The capacity to create a compelling vision and translate it into action and sustain it."

COMMUNICATION

The second skill shared by Bennis' selection of leaders is management of meaning—communications. A vision is of limited practical use if it is encased in 400 pages of wordy text or mumbled from behind a paper-packed desk. Bennis believes effective communication relies on the use of analogy, metaphor and vivid illustration as well as emotion, trust, optimism and hope.

Does Murdoch communicate his vision to those who work with and for him? This is harder to gauge, though there appears to be a high degree of loyalty among Murdoch's senior executives. The media image of Murdoch is of a taciturn Australian who occasionally vents his spleen. The reality is that he is a constant communicator. The story of the rise of the *Sun* newspaper, for example, is generally regarded as the rise of the newspaper's editors Larry Lamb and then Kelvin MacKenzie. Both strong personalities, they appeared to mold the newspaper in their own images. Yet what is notable throughout this story is the degree to which Murdoch was continually involved. Murdoch's constant phone calls at any time of the day or night serve as a constant reminder to his executives that he is on their case, knows the issues and is watching what they do.

On the second element identified by Warren Bennis, Murdoch again excels.

TRUST

The third aspect of leadership identified by Bennis is trust, which he describes as "the emotional glue that binds followers and leaders together." Leaders have to be seen as being consistent.

It is easy to conclude that Murdoch trusts his subordinates—at least to some extent. If he did not, they would be dismissed instantly. It is less easy to tell how much they trust Murdoch. Any trust comes with the caveat that anyone who has worked with Murdoch acknowledges that he is ruthless.

The somewhat surprising reality is that, given the nature of his business and the high stakes involved, Murdoch has extracted remarkable loyalty from his executives. While all no doubt have an opinion on Murdoch, few choose to share it once they have left his employ.

DEPLOYMENT OF SELF

The final common bond among the 90 leaders studied by Bennis is "deployment of self." The leaders do not glibly present charisma or time management as the essence of their success. Instead, the emphasis is on persistence and self-knowledge, taking risks, commitment and challenge but, above all, learning. "The learning person looks forward to failure or mistakes," says Bennis. "The worst problem in leadership is basically early success. There's no opportunity to learn from adversity and problems."

The conventional view of Murdoch is that he rose through the business ranks with hardly a setback. This is not the case. Murdoch has simply tended not to repeat his mistakes.

Leaders have a positive self-regard, what Bennis labels "emotional wisdom." This is characterized by an ability to accept people as they are; a capacity to approach things in terms of only the present; an ability to treat everyone, even close contacts, with courteous attention; an ability to trust others even when this seems risky; and an ability to do without constant approval and recognition.

In other words, true leaders have to be confident in themselves and in what they are doing. This is perhaps one of the most intriguing aspects of Murdoch the leader. He appears to have a very strong belief in what he is doing and how what he is doing today fits into his overall aspirations. However, the nature of his aspirations remains unclear. There is, according to some, a high degree of insecurity.

While Murdoch performs strongly against Bennis' blueprint for leadership, it is also interesting to match Murdoch against Bennis' more recent work on group working. "Greatness starts with superb people. Great groups don't exist without great leaders, but they give the lie to the persistent notion that successful institutions are the lengthened shadow of a great woman or man. It's not clear that life was ever so simple that individuals, acting alone, solved most significant problems," says Bennis.[2]

Indeed, the heroic view of the leader as the indomitable individual is now regarded by some as outdated and inappropriate. "The Lone Ranger is dead. Instead of the individual problem solver we have a new model for creative achievement. People like Steve Jobs or Walt Disney headed groups and found their own greatness in them," says Bennis. "He or she is a pragmatic dreamer, a person with an original but attainable vision. Ironically, the leader is able to realize his or her dream only if the others are free to do exceptional work. Typically, the leader is the one who recruits the others, by making the vision so palpable and seductive that they see it, too, and eagerly sign up. Inevitably, the leader has to invent a leadership style that suits the group. The standard models, especially command and control, simply don't work. The heads of groups have to act decisively, but never arbitrarily. They have to make decisions without limiting the perceived autonomy of the other participants. Devising and maintaining an atmosphere in which others can put a dent in the universe is the leader's creative act."

This profile is less obviously that of Rupert Murdoch. But there are still elements of his leadership style within it:

♦ strength of vision

♦ pragmatism

♦ ability to persuade people to sign up to his vision

♦ putting a dent in the universe—Murdoch wants to change things and shake things up.

MURDOCH THE INTERNATIONALIST

Increasingly there is an international dimension to leadership. In many ways Murdoch was an international leader ahead of his time. After all, he was leading a large global corporation in the 1970s. Since then the stakes have simply got higher and the company bigger.

Detailed and long-established research by Keith Gay and Vic Dulewicz gives rankings of competencies for chief executives of international companies.[3] They give the highest ranking to decisiveness, integrity, business sense, motivating others and vision—all elements at which Murdoch excels. Down at the bottom of the list of essential competencies are independence, appraising, written communication, detail consciousness and information collection.

Summarizing the research, Gay and Dulewicz conclude that international directors are required to "show significantly greater perspective" and strategic awareness than those who work in national companies. (This actually fits with previous research into international managerial competencies that identified strategic awareness, adaptability and sensitivity as key competencies.)

International leadership demands a broader perspective. Murdoch the chameleon is in many ways the epitome of the stateless, itinerant global executive. "Management in a global environment is increasingly affected by cultural differences," says Fons Trompenaars, whose book examines the cultural imponderables faced by managers in the global village.[4] "Basic to understanding other cultures is the awareness that culture is a series of rules and methods that a society has evolved to deal with the recurring problems it faces. They have become so basic that, like breathing, we no longer think about how we approach or resolve them," writes Trompenaars. "The international manager needs to go beyond awareness of cultural differences. He or she needs to respect these

"A model for the twenty-first century entrepreneur—a captain of industry who operates under so many flags at once that it's hard to know either where his allegiances lie or how his businesses function."

LEAD FROM THE FRONT

- *Old-fashioned leadership is not dead. Murdoch leads from the front. In the end you have to put your head on the block, make the decision and accept the risk.*

- *Vision: There is more than one way to communicate a vision. Murdoch eschews vacuous mission statements and the like, as well as bold public pronouncements. But his vision is there and is known by the people who have to deliver it.*

- *Trust: Leadership demands trust. The Western business world has been especially good at creating organizations that run without the need for trust. To fit people into organizational structures, companies have not developed them but rather limited, constrained and contained them. People have, in turn, failed to develop themselves or accept responsibility for their actions. "Responsibility is not a one-way process," says Harvard's Chris Argyris. "We are personally responsible for our behavior but, unfortunately, many companies change their parking space and not people's sense of responsibility." Leaders must build trust by encouraging others to take responsibility.*

- *Self-confidence: Rupert Murdoch is unlikely to be a reader of Stephen Covey. He could hardly be described as a flaky, self-improvement type of person. But he does possess huge internal reservoirs of self-confidence, called arrogance by some. He knows what he is capable of.*

- *Global perspectives: Murdoch was a global manager before the concept was widely practiced or understood. The world is his business playground. As such, he is one of the stateless few whose nationality is meaningless. To him, a good deal is a good deal whether it is made in Dusseldorf, Delhi or Detroit.*

> ♦ *Leaders grow companies.* Profitable growth is aston-
> ishingly elusive, according to Mercer Management
> Consulting. Between 1989 and 1994, only 271 of the
> largest 1000 U.S. public companies grew profitably.
> The remainder were shrinking, achieving "unprofitable
> growth" or cost-cutting. To explore the issues behind
> the figures Mercer gathered together 30 corporate
> leaders. Their conclusions were simple: Consistent
> growth comes from high-quality leadership. "True
> growth leaders have the vision to see coming changes
> in the marketplace and have the courage and the will
> to change their own organizations to capitalize on
> the changes." It is this will to change that is central.
> Leaders do not assume that their company has the
> right product, delivered the right way, to the right
> people, at the right cost. "True growth leaders never
> lose sight of the fact that current success is the great-
> est enemy of future success," concludes Mercer. "They
> never let themselves—or their organizations—become
> satisfied with the status quo. Staying a leader means
> never saying you've won."

differences and take advantage of diversity through reconciling cross-cultural dilemmas. The international manager reconciles cultural dilemmas."

The chameleon Murdoch actually manages this rather well. He is no longer an Australian, having renounced his citizenship to become an American. He is at ease having dinner with the Carrs to seize the *News of the World* in London, as he is on the floor of the printing room, on the streets of New York with a *Post* and a baseball cap, or in front of a journalist's computer. He is a classless global citizen, one of the first of a new breed. "It would be hard to say that the company is Australian at its core, or British, or American, because its founder, Rupert Murdoch, is an international citizen. He understands the tastes of audiences, across continents, better than any media executive," observed one profile.[5]

The *Washington Post* has described Murdoch as "a model for the twenty-first century entrepreneur—a captain of industry who operates under so many flags at once that it's hard to know either where his allegiances lie or how his businesses function."[6] The mystery works in Murdoch's behalf.

NOTES

1   Bennis, Warren.

2   Bennis, Warren.

3   Gay, Keith and Dulewicz, Victor, "Personal competencies for board directors," *Competency: The Journal of Performance through People*, Summer 1997.

4   Trompenaars, Fons, *Riding the Waves of Culture*, Nicholas Brealey, London, 1993.

5   Reif, Jessica, "Risky business: how to build a global media empire," *Red Herring*, April 1995.

6   Farhi, Paul, "Loopholes boost Murdoch's profits," *Washington Post*, December 7, 1997.

King of the Nitty-Gritty

It is often said that Murdoch, having started in one of his father's newsrooms, understands journalism. No doubt he does, but when the journalist in him comes up against the businessman, there is only one winner.

Ex-*Times* writer, Tim de Lisle

FROM GENEEN TO MURDOCH

Perhaps the manager Rupert Murdoch most resembles is the legendary ITT chief, Harold Geneen, around whom a sizeable mythology has grown. "The highest art of professional management requires the literal ability to *smell a real fact* from all others—and, moreover, to have the temerity, intellectual curiosity, guts and/or plain impoliteness, if necessary, to be sure that what you do have is indeed what we will call an *unshakeable fact*," said Geneen.

Geneen joined the board of ITT in 1959 and set about turning the company into the world's greatest conglomerate. His basic organizational strategy was that diversification was a source of strength. There was nothing halfhearted in Geneen's pursuit of diversity. Under Geneen, ITT bought companies as addictively as Imelda Marcos once bought shoes. ITT's spending spree amounted to 350 companies and included Avis

Rent-A-Car, Sheraton Hotels, Continental Baking and Levitt & Sons among many others. By 1970 ITT was composed of 400 separate companies operating in 70 countries.

The ragbag collection of names was a managerial nightmare. Keeping the growing array of companies under control was a complex series of financial checks and targets. Geneen managed them with intense vigor. Few other executives could have done so, but he brought a unique single-mindedness to the task. As part of his formula, every month more than fifty executives flew to Brussels to spend four days poring over the figures. "I want no surprises," announced Geneen. He hoped to make people "as predictable and controllable as the capital resources they must manage." While others would have watched as the deck of cards fell to the ground, Geneen kept adding more cards, while managing to know the pressures and stresses each was under.

Facts were the lifeblood of the expanding ITT— and executives sweated blood in their pursuit. Geneen's managerial approach was candidly explained by ITT in its 1971 annual report: "More than 200 days a year are devoted to management meetings at various organizational levels throughout the world. In these meetings in New York, Brussels, Hong Kong, Buenos Aires, decisions are made based on logic—the business logic that results in making decisions which are almost inevitable because all the facts on which the decisions must be based are available. The function of the planning and the meetings is to force the logic out into the open where its value and need are seen by all."

By sheer force of personality, Geneen's approach worked. (More cynically, you could say that

ITT was a success within the parameters created by Geneen.) Between 1959 and 1977 ITT's sales went from $765 million to nearly $28 billion. Earnings went from $29 million to $562 million and earnings per share rose from $1 to $4.20. Geneen stepped down as chief executive in 1977 and as chairman in 1979.

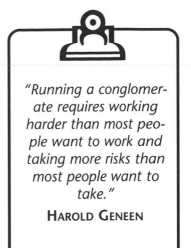

"Running a conglomerate requires working harder than most people want to work and taking more risks than most people want to take."

HAROLD GENEEN

ITT rapidly disintegrated following Geneen's departure. Indeed, the writing was on the wall before that—the company's profits fell in 1974 and 1975. "Running a conglomerate requires working harder than most people want to work and taking more risks than most people want to take," said Geneen. His followers were unable to sustain his uniquely driven working style. The underside of ITT was exposed: It had worked with the CIA in Chile and been involved in offering bribes. The deck of cards tumbled.

To Geneen, the fall in ITT's fortunes simply served to validate his methods and philosophy. "After I left, the company veered on to a new course, emphasizing consolidation rather than growth ... Often, I have felt the stab of frustration and regret, wondering what might have been," he reflected in his 1997 book.[1] It was curiously fitting that in the month of Harold Geneen's death, ITT was taken over.

MASTERING THE DETAIL

The ethos of Harold Geneen was that while leadership is the broad brush, management is detail. Rupert

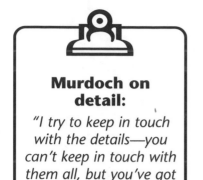
Murdoch believes likewise. In the manner of a modern Geneen, Murdoch manages more detail than virtually any person alive. "I try to keep in touch with the details—you can't keep in touch with them all, but you've got to have a feel for what's going on. I also look at the product daily. That doesn't mean you interfere, but it's important occasionally to show the ability to be involved. It shows you understand what's happening."

Rupert Murdoch was brought up on a diet of newspapers. He understands the processes and, indeed, has played a leading part in changing them. Being involved in newspapers was a natural thing for him to do. He saw his father's newspapers in operation. He worked as a copy editor at the *Daily Express*. He has written and subbed, and knows the traditional printing process inside out. These skills played an important part in the early development of his career.

This is not to say that Murdoch is a great sub-editor, headline writer, editor or journalist. He is not, but he knows the essence of these jobs. He knows what makes a great editor and he knows what makes a great populist story.

The great thing about Murdoch's career is that his basic knowledge of the newspaper industry was fully utilized to give him the financial clout to gain entry to the bigger stakes of global media. He has used every ounce of his inside knowledge and made it work. Now he is involved in a game where the stakes are incredibly high and the knowledge of the participants is limited. It is limited by the fact that Murdoch and a handful of others are betting on the future. They are investing in technology they don't even know will work to tap into markets that won't exist until sometime in the future.

Murdoch keeps up on what's happening through ten-day stints every three months at every division. This face-to-face contact means that he keeps abreast of the performance of his huge organization as much as is humanly possible. He is there— or executives feel that he is there. "But when states are acquired in a country differing in language, customs, or laws, there are difficulties, and good fortune and great energy are needed to hold them, and one of the greatest and most real helps would be that he who has acquired them should go and reside there . . . Because if one is on the spot, disorders are seen as they spring up, and one can quickly remedy them; but if one is not at hand, they are heard of only when they are great, and then one can no longer remedy them," advised Niccolò Machiavelli many centuries ago. The value of being on the spot can never be underestimated.

Of course, modern technology means that you can be everywhere. One element of how Murdoch uses technology was described by Andrew Neil as "the brutal telephone terrorism by which he rules his worldwide empire, enabling him to strike fear at any time even in his most peripheral domains."[2] Translated, Murdoch uses the phone a lot. "He has a proprietorial finger in every pie and on every pulse. No respecter of time zones, he rings and rouses his senior executives at all hours for detailed telephone briefings. He may ring off without saying goodbye," noted one article.[3]

This behavior is generally interpreted as interference. If commitment to detail is not backed by knowledge, it is interference. The difference is that Murdoch knows. Some of his most experienced former employees reject the notion that he directly interferes. Harold Evans, former editor of the *Sunday Times* and the *Times* under Murdoch, is among them. "He is not a miniaturist. He creates an aura," wrote Evans in his biography.[4] Murdoch's sheer presence has an effect on people. They get the message.

"He has a proprietorial finger in every pie and on every pulse."

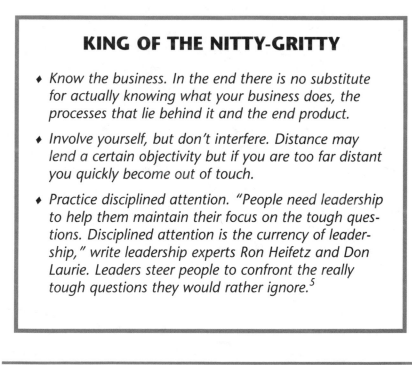

KING OF THE NITTY-GRITTY

+ *Know the business. In the end there is no substitute for actually knowing what your business does, the processes that lie behind it and the end product.*

+ *Involve yourself, but don't interfere. Distance may lend a certain objectivity but if you are too far distant you quickly become out of touch.*

+ *Practice disciplined attention. "People need leadership to help them maintain their focus on the tough questions. Disciplined attention is the currency of leadership," write leadership experts Ron Heifetz and Don Laurie. Leaders steer people to confront the really tough questions they would rather ignore.[5]*

NOTES

1   Geneen, Harold, *The Synergy Myth*, St. Martin's Press, London, 1997.

2   Neil, Andrew, "Rupert the fear," *The Guardian*, March 2, 1998.

3   Parkes, Christopher and Newman, Cathy, "Dealmaker's dilemma," *Financial Times*, April 25–26, 1998.

4   Evans, Harold, Buckland, Gail and Baker, Kevin, *The American Century*, Alfred A. Knopf, Inc., New York, 1998.

5   Heifetz, Ronald A. and Laurie, Donald L., "The work of leadership," *Harvard Business Review*, January–February 1997.

6

DNA Marketing

Good companies will meet needs; great companies will create markets. Market leadership is gained by envisioning new products, services, lifestyles, and ways to raise living standards. There is a vast difference between companies that offer me-too products and those that create new product and service values not even imagined by the marketplace. Ultimately, marketing at its best is about value creation and raising the world's living standards.

PHILIP KOTLER

MURDOCH THE MARKETER

Rupert Murdoch has marketing in his DNA. Rupert Murdoch's marketing genius is basic, decidedly unesoteric. It is base and hard-selling. It is unsophisticated and yet hugely successful. To Murdoch, marketing is the hard sell and little else. Forget fanciful notions of relationship marketing and brand awareness.

Murdoch's marketing style is epitomized by the *Sun* newspaper—"The paper which gets you up in the morning." With its steady stream of *double entendres*, terrible puns, horror stories, gross simplifications and nationalistic nonsense, the *Sun* is the benchmark against which tabloids the world over are judged. It is a triumph of its genre, of style over substance, of crassness over sensitivity. It is difficult to put down. Following George Michael's arrest in a Los Angeles public toilet, the *Sun's* headline was, "Zip me up before you go-go." Another headline was the unlikely, but intriguing, "I was Carlos the Jackal's driving instructor." More typically, European Community commissioner Jacques Delors was greeted with the welcoming headline, "Up your Delors." A more recent classic is "Camilla sleeps at the Palace," supposedly revealing the sleeping arrangements of Prince Charles' friend. Other newspapers in Murdoch's stable have followed suit. "Headless body in topless bar" is a staple headline from the *New York Post*. Populism is infectious. Not long after being bought by Murdoch, the *Sunday Times* published the forged Hitler diaries in 1983.

"There is nothing that Murdoch has touched in his brilliant career that he has not taken ruthlessly downmarket," noted Jurek Martin commenting on Murdoch's acquisition of the Los Angles Dodgers.[1] To this common criticism, Murdoch commonly retorts with characteristic relish: "You know, William Shakespeare wrote for the masses."

What can be forgotten is that Murdoch knows his customers very well. For a globetrotting billionaire he has a keen idea of what people like and dislike.

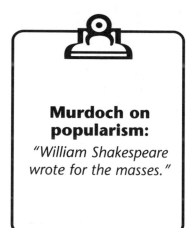

Murdoch on popularism:

"William Shakespeare wrote for the masses."

Other aspects of traditional marketing are also utilized by Murdoch with characteristic *brio*. Murdoch's newspapers brought the humble art of promotion into the twentieth century. They turned it into a sophisticated tool with high stakes. When Robert Maxwell came up with the idea of including bingo games in his newspapers, Murdoch was the first to create a bingo millionaire. A bingo battle ensued. We can thank Murdoch for a host of other crass and cheerful promotions. Even the *Times* offered a bingo competition at one point.

Murdoch is also very keen on price competitiveness. His is not the world of premium brands. For example, he ignited a ruthless price war in the U.K. newspaper industry. In September 1993 the circulations of the *Times* and of its competitor, the *Independent,* were both around 350,000. Murdoch cut the price of the *Times* from 45 pence to 30 pence. The *Independent,* curiously, raised its price to prove it was above such cheap tricks. In the first half of 1994, the *Times'* circulation rose by around 40 percent, to 500,000. The *Independent's* circulation fell to 275,000 and it teetered on the brink of collapse. Such aggressive price cutting is par for the course. It is hardly a sophisticated strategy—though there may have been some enjoyment for Murdoch in proving that *Times* readers are as susceptible to price as anyone else.

Murdoch's price cutting does not always work— the *Sun's* price war with its archrival the *Daily Mirror* appeared to make little difference.

Hard sell follows hard sell. Murdoch does not care. Selling is selling. There is no embarrassment. That's what businesses do. If Microsoft wants to buy up the *Times* and use it to promote Windows 95, it can do so because it is good business.

Similarly, Murdoch does not like to miss any chance to market his companies. In Twentieth Century Fox's *Independence Day,* characters watch the European channel Sky News. Both companies are owned by Murdoch. The fact that characters in the U.S. are watching a European channel is regarded as incidental. This sort of thing—less subliminal usual-ly—happens all the time. Murdoch-owned newspapers plug films produced by Murdoch companies. For a while, it appeared that Murdoch papers could write about nothing other than the Murdoch film, *Titanic*. The genius of cross-media ownership is that the per-mutations are endless. A film can be reviewed for an upmarket audience in the *Times* and for a different audience in the *Sun*.

The trouble with this arrangement is that notions of journalistic independence go out the win-dow. Rupert Murdoch does not see this as a quandary. It is human nature to promote your own products. Heavy-handed, product-oriented synergies simply make the most of the organization.

Others are not so sure. "Rupert's Rule appears to be that all lines are permeable. And the notion of synergy, so logical and beneficial in many commer-cial enterprises, takes on a cynical and even malevo-lent cast when the corporation is a multimedia empire with Murdoch at the helm," said the *Columbia Journalism Review*.[2]

MARKET DRIVEN

Crass it may be, but Murdoch is a brilliant marketing man. News Corp is genuinely market driven. Wharton's George S. Day provides an explanation of what it means to be market driven.

First, he says that firms that fail to become mar-ket driven usually fall prey to three traps. Some become "self-centered." The archetypal example of this is what happened to IBM during the 1980s. It became distant from its customers. Customer information was poorly captured and distributed. Senior managers became ever more distant from what was happening in the marketplace. In addition, its undoubted centers of excellence existed in isolation. IBM continued to sustain superb standards, but lacked any means of delivering such excellence on a broader scale. IBM also began to concentrate on cost reduction to achieve short-term financial results rather than on long-term development.

Unfortunately, the next pitfall identified by George Day, "the customer compulsion trap," is also epitomized by IBM—though this time in the early 1990s. In effect, IBM sought to redress the balance by listening to each and every one of its customers. The result was confusion and disillusionment, which leads to the final trap: skepticism. Companies can regard customers as an unwelcome distraction, arguing that customers should be led rather than followed.

Day concludes that the route to becoming market driven is likely to involve a number of characteristics: offering superior solutions and experiences; focusing on superior customer value; converting satisfaction to loyalty; energizing and retaining employees; anticipating competitors' moves; viewing marketing as an investment, not a cost; and nurturing and leveraging brands as assets. In the end, the companies that succeed will have some—though not all—of these characteristics. Most strike a chord with what News Corp does so well.

Similarly, marketing guru Philip Kotler provides three key aphorisms for shaping the future:

♦ Invest in the future—"Companies pay too much attention to the cost of doing something. They should worry more about the cost of not doing it."

- Move fast—"Every company should work hard to obsolete its own product line . . . before its competitors do."
- Excel at everything you do—"Your company does not belong in any market where it can't be the best."

The message is that marketing must become part of the mainstream of all an organization's activities. The word *marketing* is notably absent from Tom Peters' exhortations for organizations to become customer-oriented. The reason is simple—everyone must be involved in marketing in the same way that everyone must be dedicated to quality. In the best organizations marketing is left unsaid, but not undone. Once again, News Corp's focus on moving fast, creating the future and leading the field rather than following, marks it apart as a marketing driven and market driven organization.

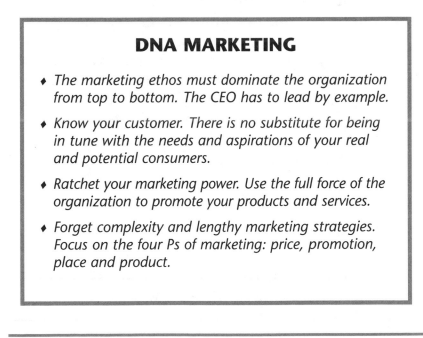

DNA MARKETING

- *The marketing ethos must dominate the organization from top to bottom. The CEO has to lead by example.*

- *Know your customer. There is no substitute for being in tune with the needs and aspirations of your real and potential consumers.*

- *Ratchet your marketing power. Use the full force of the organization to promote your products and services.*

- *Forget complexity and lengthy marketing strategies. Focus on the four Ps of marketing: price, promotion, place and product.*

NOTES

1   Martin, Jurek, "Foul ball," *Salon*, March 26, 1998.

2   Baker, Russ, "Murdoch's mean machine," *Columbia Journalism Review*, May/June 1998.

Speed Freaks

In this business, there are two kinds of people,
really, the quick and the dead.

MICHAEL DELL

BE FAST; BE FIRST

In 1959 Murdoch's Southern TV went on the air. Despite a fire rendering the planned studio unusable, Southern beat archrival Channel 7 to be the first to broadcast. Murdoch had insisted that the race be won—and doing so involved using chicken wire, sewing machines and blankets to rig up a makeshift studio.

"Not for him a cumbersome board of directors and the endless second-guessing of other executives. Even when he nearly put the company into bankruptcy in 1991, his bankers reckoned that no one else could do a better job of running the rescued empire," says media analyst Matthew Horsman. "The resultant, and astonishing, freedom has allowed Rupert Murdoch to make lightning moves—as when he stole Star TV, the Asian pay-TV company, out from under the nose of the slower moving Pearson, or when Murdoch himself was allowed on News Corp's behalf to agree the broad terms of a merger between his Sky Television and British Satellite Broadcasting back in 1990."[1]

Murdoch has long recognized that the first one into new markets has a valuable and potentially lucrative head start. This fact of corporate life has never been truer. No matter what business you are in, life is becoming more competitive. Companies are faced with having to keep abreast of product developments on a global scale. No matter what your resources, this is virtually impossible. Geographical and physical divides have disappeared. There are fewer barriers to the flow of information. If you improve a product in Beijing, thanks to technology, someone in Baltimore will soon be able to find out—or vice versa. (It is notable that in this new world order, the threat and the opportunity are inextricably linked. Global accessibility is both the opportunity and the source of potential competition.)

Technological change means that products are continually enhanced in order to survive. Product life cycles are perpetually shortening. Photographic cameras, for example, have a life span as short as six months. The number of models on the market grows unceasingly as competitors avidly copy each other's innovations. This desperate race with no end makes it clear that products still matter. But having autofocus or the latest gimmick is the price of entry rather than the winning ticket.

Murdoch on speed:

"The winners will be those who capitalize quickly on changing opportunities. The challenge is to move early and innovate often."

The daunting truth is that copying products has never been easier. Any company that protects patents and copyrights is among the surest bets to become a booming business in the new millennium. Goods that are close substitutes for each other in the customers' eyes are more generally available than ever before. Virtually any product on earth can be speedily replicated.

In financial services, any new product—whether it be an account for the elderly or a more flexible mortgage—is copied almost instantly. There is a constant stream of products and services as old ones are tinkered with, replaced or revamped, and entirely new ones are introduced. In one year the U.K.-based bank NatWest introduced 240 new products or improvements to existing products. There is no longer anything particularly unusual in this.

In industry after industry, today's bright ideas quickly become permanent fixtures. Today's leading edge is tomorrow's condition of entry. Competitive advantage tends not to be sustainable for very long—and this period is becoming ever shorter in duration. "In this business, by the time you realize you're in trouble, it's too late to save yourself," says Bill Gates. Intel chief Andy Grove has argued that in this environment "only the paranoid survive," explaining, "You have no choice but to operate in a world shaped by globalization and the information revolution. There are two options: adapt or die. The new environment dictates two rules: first, everything happens faster; second, anything that can be done will be done, if not by you, then by someone else, somewhere. Let there be no misunderstandings: these changes lead to a less kind, less gentle, and less predictable workplace.

As managers in such a workplace, you need to develop a higher tolerance for disorder."

In News Corp's 1997 Annual Report, Rupert Murdoch acknowledged the new reality: "The borderless world opened up to us by the digital information age will afford huge challenges and limitless opportunities in the years ahead. It will continue to be a period of turmoil in terms of changes in technology and challenges posed by regulatory authorities around the world. The winners will be those who capitalize quickly on changing opportunities. The challenge is to move early and innovate often. This is not always a comfortable path, but it is the only one which will lead News Corporation to success in the global market of the twenty-first century."

ORGANIZE TO MOVE FAST

The result of this trend is that organizations like News Corp need to be geared toward moving fast to seize the short-lived advantage.

This means that companies must minimize their hierarchies. Throughout the twentieth century, corporate hierarchies have spawned greater costs rather than improved productivity or higher quality products and services. During the last decade, the vast numbers of middle and junior managers have been recognized by a large number of organizations as a costly indulgence. (Noticeably, Murdoch and News Corp actually steered clear of the downsizing epidemic. They didn't need to trim an already lean staff.)

Clearly, the most obvious side effect of a burdensome hierarchy is slow decision making. If every decision has to be filtered through ten lines of hierarchy, no decision is likely to be made quickly. In the past this was not a significant impediment to commercial success. In the 1960s and 1970s companies did not have to move quickly—markets were there, usually national in nature, and evolving at a slow pace. Now, with emphasis on the speed of product development and delivery, it is crucial that decisions can be made immediately. For example, 3M requires that 30 percent of each of its units' sales must be generated by products introduced in the last four years.

The obvious conclusion drawn by companies throughout the world is that layers of management need to be eradicated. Instead of pyramids of middle managers rarely communicating with one another, the onus is on project teams and cross-functional working.

Behind this is the inescapable impact of information technology (IT). IT enables managers to communicate more effectively than ever before. It is not constrained by hierarchical structures. Instead, it allows managers to cut through hierarchy to communicate with the people they need to communicate with, no matter where they are positioned in the organization—geographically or hierarchically. Because as many middle management jobs had become functions for filtering and directing information, they are effectively redundant.

Times are changing. But that does not mean that managers and their organizations are necessarily moving as quickly as the trends that engulf them.

News Corp is a hybrid organization, not a traditional top-heavy conglomerate, but not a freewheeling networked organization either. As Henley Management College's Ian Turner has pointed out, the role of the center in the new organization linked by technology and involved in a multitude of partnerships and alliances is crucial.[2] Such network organizations require a high level of trust—often not much in evidence in the business world. Also, splitting up an organization into a myriad of autonomous profit centers provokes a logical question: Why have an organization at all? The balance is a precarious one and the role of the center will be perennially challenged. But competing in many mass markets demands the sales volumes generated by global operations. Truly independent profit centers may make a company vulnerable to globally organized competitors.

News Corp straddles various organizational forms. "The extraordinary thing about News Corporation . . . is just how illogical the whole appears," said one analyst.[3] What makes it work is the energy of Rupert Murdoch. Without him it is difficult to see how it could survive.

THINK FAST; ACT FASTER

Even so, Murdoch is one of the executives who long ago realized the deficiencies and limitations of a hierarchical organization. There is a strong entrepreneurial feel to News Corp's activities. News Corp moves fast. "You can't build a strong corporation with a lot of committees and a board that has to be consulted every turn. You have to be able to make decisions on your own," says Murdoch.[4]

Moving fast affects all aspects of the business. Whether it is looking at taking over another company or recruiting new staff, News Corp moves quickly. The magazine *Mirabella* was created when Conde Nast ditched *Vogue* editor Grace Mirabella in 1988. While others considered what to do and how Mirabella could fit in, Murdoch was speedily on the phone offering her the chance to create something new, rather than just another job.

In moving fast and seizing the opportunity, Murdoch behaves like the owner of a much smaller business. "Murdoch is one of the world's greatest entrepreneurs. In terms of the ability to manage great risk, which really is the definition of an entrepreneur, I don't think anyone in the world is better at it than Rupert. Without any question," says ex-Fox chief Barry Diller. "He follows and exploits opportunity better than anyone alive and with no support system to depend upon other than himself."[5]

One of Murdoch's important realizations is that the connections between businesses, ideas, products, services and people are now far more commonplace. Clearly it is self-serving continually to refer to products or services offered by other parts of your organization. But we notice it more easily because it is now so easily done. Mass media means mass advertising; mass media also means that our reference points, the connections between us and ideas, are many more than ever previously existed.

Connectivity, as it is labeled by Chris Meyer and Stan Davis in their book, *Blur*, is the order of the day.[6] Understanding connectivity is like coming to terms with the childhood revelation that we are all, somewhere along the line, related. A whole new family suddenly emerges before you go on to ponder the awful impossibility of it all. In the information economy mapped out by Davis and Meyer, small things are connected in a myriad of ways to create a "complex adaptive system." Instantaneous, multiple connections are speeding the economy up and, more critically, changing the way it works.

The trouble is that the connections are so many and so complex that they can bring things to a grinding, inexplicable halt. "The stock market crash of October 1987 was caused by computerized trades, none of which were linked explicitly. The damage was done by the interaction of independent investor instructions—a kind of connected network of trading programs," write Davis and Meyer. So the stock market crash was not a frenzy of capitalism, but a connectivity short circuit.

The question must be whether News Corp and Rupert Murdoch can sustain their network of connections in the face of inevitable short circuits.

SPEED FREAKS

♦ Move fast. There is no substitute for making decisions and acting upon them faster than your competitors. Sloth is for the market losers. Only the fast survive.

♦ Organize accordingly. Big and unwieldy it may seem, but News Corp is geared for action. The downside is that action relies too heavily on Murdoch's say-so.

♦ Eliminate hierarchy. "The number of levels of authority should be kept to a minimum," said early management theorist Chester Barnard. Every level of hierarchy is another barrier to a decision being made.

♦ Build from connectivity. It is only by accepting and seeking to utilize the mass of connections now available that you can compete.

NOTES

1   Horsman, Matthew, "After Rupert, what?" *The Guardian*, April 27, 1998.

2   Turner, Ian, "Strategy in virtual communities," *Manager Update*, Spring 1996.

3   Horsman, Mathew, "After Rupert, what?"

4   Safire, William and Safire, Leonard, *Leadership: A Treasury of Great Quotations for Everybody Who Aspires to Succeed as a Leader,* Simon & Schuster, New York, 1990.

5   Farhi, Paul, "Murdoch, all business," *Washington Post*, February 12, 1995.

6   Davis, Stan and Meyer, Chris, *Blur*, Capstone, Oxford, 1998.

Think Tomorrow Today

Tomorrow is our permanent address.

MARSHALL MCLUHAN

IMAGINE THE FUTURE CONTINUOUSLY

Rupert Murdoch does not look like a far-sighted visionary. In his crumpled suits, he looks like an executive who has crossed the globe a few too many times. Yet his career has been built on envisioning the future. "He is a man with relentless, unceasing drive and energy and a brilliant flair for spotting trends in popular culture," wrote William Shawcross. "From the 1950s on, trends surfaced in the United States, and were then exported abroad, at least to the English-speaking world. Murdoch understood instinctively the allure of America to the rest of the world."[1]

Murdoch spots trends, bets on them, and then sticks with it.

"He is a man with relentless, unceasing drive and energy and a brilliant flair for spotting trends in popular culture."

Sometimes it works. Other times it unravels in front of him. His dream of a global satellite network, for example, appears (in the middle of 1998) to be unraveling. The imagined intergalactic fleet of satellites, a cosmic armada, has so far failed to materialize. But that does not mean it will never materialize. Murdoch will undoubtedly stick with it, seeking out new deals to make it work—even if it goes the same way as the Spanish Armada. Look at his persistence with Sky in the U.K. News Corp's 40 percent stake in BSkyB is now worth in excess of $6 billion. ("BSkyB is one of the best businesses I've ever seen," said one commentator.)

So Murdoch's first future-watching skill is that he actually thinks about the future. This, you might think, is no great skill at all. But it is something that executives are notably poor at doing. They tend, instead, to be consumed by the moment. Managers are bogged down in the nitty-gritty of the present—according to Gary Hamel and C.K. Prahalad they spend less than three percent of their time looking to the future. Similarly, research by Henry Mintzberg found that managers were slaves to the moment, moving from task to task with every move dogged by another diversion, another call. The median time spent on any one issue was a mere nine minutes. Murdoch's gift is to be able to absorb the detail of the present while still casting an eye over the parapets to the future.

He seeks to understand what has been and to make sense of the available data and underlying patterns. What could

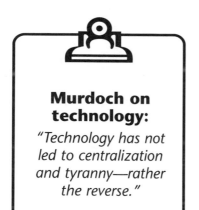

Murdoch on technology:

"Technology has not led to centralization and tyranny—rather the reverse."

the patterns tell him? Most executives are attracted to patterns that fit their worldview. They confirm their prejudices—though take care to label their prejudices as strategies. They seek out trends and statistics that support their ideas and overlook the rest.

In contrast, Murdoch is sensitive to faint signals in the internal and external environments. He sees things coming, once again a matter of intuition as well as analysis. He asks, What if?

THINK LONG-TERM

Rupert Murdoch plays a long game. He subsidized the *Australian* for 20 years and is always willing to outbid a competitor for something that might reap dividends in the future—look at his acquisition of the rights to broadcast NFL football.

Look also at the way he has courted the Chinese. In his mind 1.3 billion consumers in an untapped market cannot be wrong. As a result, the BBC was ousted from his Asian Star satellite system. The corporation's offense was broadcasting programs critical of the Chinese government. Murdoch also divested his interest in the *South China Morning Post*, a frequent critic of the Chinese authorities. He has published sycophantic books about Deng Xiaoping and got himself into a PR muddle when he pulled out of the Chris Patten book deal. This is hardly subtle, but it is a sign of how much China means to Murdoch.

It has not been plain sailing, however. Murdoch's investment in Star has been a nightmare with heavy losses reported. With costs of $250 million and revenues of $150 million, it is a long way from being profitable. Yet again, he shows all the signs of being willing to stick with it to find the gold at the end. And once again, Murdoch is displaying his pragmatism. Star relies on the goodwill of the Chinese government, the last remaining Communist superpower. Unless the Chinese government backs Star, it will never take off in the country. One way or another, Murdoch has to gain governmental backing.

Murdoch has been jockeying for position in typical fashion. Each deal pushes the Chinese government in his direction. News Corp, for example, invested in a share of Phoenix Satellite Television, which specializes in China-friendly broadcasting.

Murdoch's long-term perspectives are reminiscent of those adopted by the Japanese. It is reputed that when the Japanese were trying to take over the operations of Yosemite National Park in California, the first thing they submitted was a 250-year business plan. Initially, after they had got up off the floor, the thoughts of the American managers turned to a horrific (or reassuring, depending on your point of view) statistic—250 years is 1000 quarterly reports. "Americans tend to think about the improvement of the next quarter, while the Japanese do not ignore the short-term but tend to place it in the context of the long-term future. That is as close as managers can get to reconciling different time frames," says cultural guru Fons Trompenaars.[2] Murdoch combines the Eastern long view with the problem-solving skills of Western managers.

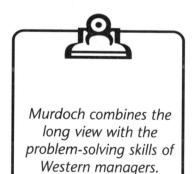

Murdoch combines the long view with the problem-solving skills of Western managers.

THE FUTURE WILL BE DIFFERENT

It is not simply that Murdoch looks to the future, spots trends and backs them. Crucially, he realizes that the future will be different. This sounds obvious. It is. But think what would have happened if Murdoch had imagined in 1960 that the future would be very much like the present. If he had thought along those lines he would be running a newspaper empire with no other interests. He would probably own virtually every newspaper in the world by now and be watching as circulation gradually fell in the face of alternative forms of entertainment.

The future will be different. Today's rules will not apply tomorrow—no matter what tomorrow brings. What is safe and acceptable today is tomorrow's disaster. Asbestos was considered to be safe 40 years ago.

Leadership researchers Randall White and Philip Hodgson argue that, in practice, faced with the unknowable and uncertain, organizations follow three options: ignore, contain or adapt.[3]

Ignore: Deny the data or declare it to be irrelevant

There is always tension between past patterns or achievements and future possibilities. Organizations and their managers must learn to embrace and accept those tensions. Unfortunately, in practice they too often ignore the tension and say, "We will increase what we did last year by ten percent." They regard the future as linear, not chaotic. They assume next year will be the same as this year.

In reality, the corporate capacity for self-delusion is enormous. Witness the oil price rises of the 1970s when the oil companies sought to carry on with business as normal. Or GM. Or IBM. The list is long. (See Murdoch's 10th secret for how he ensures that News Corp does not surrender to complacency.)

In a risk-averse environment, the emphasis is on protecting assets, market share and the organization as a whole rather than remaining open to learning. To do anything else is to take a risk. Most companies concentrate on protection in the present rather than preparation for the future. They protect their assets and protect their ability to learn, grow and change. Often, protection concentrates on resources and assets. Organizations that follow this course constrain the development of these aspects of their business. They believe they have too much to lose and, once you have something to lose, fear takes over. As companies grow, protective instincts tend to expand at a similar rate.

Assuming the future will turn out like the past provides disappointment after disappointment. Executives are trained to ignore these. Look at annual reports. Have you ever read a corporate annual report that offers a bleak perspective on the future? Despite the fact that companies are impermanent legal manifestations liable to be taken over, hit the rocks or become subsumed into another elusive entity, senior executives rarely admit this is the case. (The only glorious exception is Warren Buffett's annual letter to Berkshire Hathaway shareholders, which is refreshingly frank and honest.)

If the future doesn't turn out to be the same as the past, executives quickly—and skillfully—claim that this could not have been anticipated or prepared for. But what if it could?

Preparing for the unknowable is not as impossible as the phraseology suggests. But first you need to learn what worked and didn't work in the past and be willing to do things differently in the future.

Contain: Acknowledge the data, but decide to do nothing

The second response to the unknowable future is to contain; this is organizational stupor—"We know about that, but let's wait and see."

In the modern corporation, managers can gamble blindly, assuming tomorrow's result will be the same as yesterday's, or they can engage in an intelligence competition. Often they carry on as before, content to let things be if they are controlled and contained.

Adapt: Acknowledge the data and act

The organizations that adapt tend to take action that falls into four categories: Internally they prepare and protect; externally they seek out patterns and possibilities. Patterns come from analysis of past data; possibilities are derived by taking past patterns and imposing them on future data. Patterns are not used to make predictions. Instead they are used as a testing ground to help prepare for the widest possible range of futures. Companies are then in the position to make what decisions they can—not necessarily the right ones—to achieve the best possible fit between the organization and its environment.

THINK TOMORROW TODAY

♦ *Invest time in considering the future. The common retort to this is: How can executives look to the future when they are worrying about how they can get through this month? How can they look far ahead when even the immediate future is uncertain? Yet that is what they are expected to do. That is what they have to do. They must consolidate and declare ambitious growth objectives. They must focus on local markets as well as internal cooperation. They must improve their individual effectiveness while becoming great team players. They must continue being active while increasing the amount of time spent in reflecting. These pressures are enormous and paradoxical. In the Western world we have tended to shy away from such paradoxes, and yet the leaders of tomorrow will need to be fluent in handling paradoxes—to move from situations that provide either/or alternatives to ones with both/and solutions.*

♦ *Embrace technology. As Murdoch recognized long ago, the future is technology. "The nerds have won," as Tom Peters has put it. Rupert Murdoch may talk about satellites and global networks and the like, but he is hardly a computer nerd. He is no techno lover. He simply loves anything that enables him to run his business more cheaply or that opens up entirely new markets. "Technology has not led to centralization and tyranny—rather the reverse," he says.[4] Murdoch regards technology as a positive force rather than simply a negative means of reducing headcount. As Harvard's Shoshana Zuboff points out in her book,* In the Age of the Smart Machine,[5] *companies have regarded IT as a means of reducing staff numbers through the automation of jobs. The trouble is that the jobs that have been automated out of existence are often those that involve direct contact with customers. Zuboff argues that instead of automating tasks, IT's job should be to "informate" people—an ungainly, but apposite, word combining inform and educate. By regarding IT as a numbers and cost-cutting mechanism, organizations fail to optimize its full potential, which goes far beyond cost reduction. Murdoch does not make that mistake.*

NOTES

1   Shawcross, William, *Murdoch*, Chatto & Windus, London, 1992.

2   Trompenaars, Fons, "Cultural factors of international management," *Financial Times Handbook of Management* (ed. Crainer, S.), FT/Pitman, London, 1995.

3   White, Randall et al., *The Future of Leadership: Riding the Corporate Rapids into the 21st Century*, Pitman U.K., 1996.

4   Murdoch, Rupert, "The century of networking," The 11th Annual John Bonython Lecture, Melbourne, Australia, October 20, 1994.

5   Zuboff, Shoshana, *In the Age of the Smart Machine*, Basic Books, New York, 1989.

Ambition Never Dies

People think that at the top there isn't much room.
They tend to think of it as an Everest. My message
is that there is tons of room at the top.

MARGARET THATCHER

AMBITION NEVER DIES

News Corporation is Rupert Murdoch's company. Of that there is little doubt even though he owns just over 30 percent of it. Rarely has one man dominated such a vast organization with such efficiency. Speak about the company's strategy and you are, in effect, speaking about Murdoch's own strategy.

In terms of management practice, this is a dangerous policy to follow. Can one man carry such a hugely diverse organization? Murdoch does so by sheer force of personality and his high-octane energy levels. One business analyst noted: "Maybe no single person can take over all the reins if and when Rupert retires. There may be no one who can run the businesses like Rupert."[1]

In his late sixties, Murdoch continues to work like a young man. His drive remains apparently undiminished. While his competitors toss and turn with worry, he sleeps a mere three hours per night. "The world is speeding up and Rupert speeds up as well," one of his associates noted. "He has the super-human energy of a 35-year old," said one of his colleagues.[2]

Leaders are energetic. They have to be. Margaret Thatcher slept four hours a night and rose to pore over yet more government papers. IBM's Lou Gerstner is renowned for his energy (and sleep) levels. Top executives travel constantly and yet still emerge from the arrivals lounge looking fresh, armed with a report they've just written somewhere over the ocean. "He was like a whirlwind coming into the room," Anna Murdoch said of meeting Rupert. David Campbell of the Center for Creative Leadership finds over and over that effective leaders and high energy go hand in hand on his Leadership Inventory.

Energy is a prerequisite for the job. The mistake is to think that Murdoch's secret is quantity rather than quality. Maximizing energy is much more than running fast or working harder. Anyone can work 16 hours a day. The world is full of hard-working executives who have mortgaged their future health against their current working days. However, how you spend your time and how you enthuse others is more important. Quality is vital; quantity is no longer a competitive advantage. In fact, executives who pin their faith simply on working harder are taking a route to burnout and disenchantment.

Rupert Murdoch's energy leads him to question what others assume. The message is that leaders have to dig deep and deeper and deeper still. They must peel away the layers. Executives must look for problems to solve. And then there is another problem, and another. "Your products are always gonna be obsolete so you'd better enjoy doing the next version," says Bill Gates. "It's like pinball—if you play a good game, the reward is that you get to play another game—there is no ultimate gain."[3]

It helps, of course, if you actually regard what you do as important. The job must matter. Why else is Jack Welch running GE after a triple bypass or Michael Eisner still at Disney after his heart attack? Why is Rupert Murdoch still traveling the globe when he is nearly 70? "I love ... working with the ideas of the world, playing in the theater of the mind," he says. "At News Corporation, we're interested in ideas, not just dollars and cents, and interestingly, that seems to work too."[4]

For such leaders, financial motivation is limited. Billionaires tend not to worry quite so much about their next paycheck. They are not angelic figures who regard financial rewards as unimportant. They expect to be well rewarded, but look beyond the narrow motivation of money alone. Paul Allen, Microsoft founder, recalling the day he and Bill Gates realized they had shipped one million copies of BASIC, says: "We were marveling that, wow, a million people were using our code to do God-knows-what number of interesting things. That was such a gratifying thing to realize, that you have been able to affect other people's lives in a positive way."[5]

It is difficult to determine whether Rupert Murdoch has such emotions—or aspirations about the impact of his work. His public pronouncements occasionally suggest that he has. "I love the free market. It's certainly been very good to me. I think you'd have to admit, it's been very good to the world," he has said.[6] Elsewhere he has talked of the social benefits of satellite broadcasting: "Satellite broadcasting makes it possible for information-hungry residents of many closed societies to bypass state-controlled television."[7]

The question of what drives Rupert Murdoch has occupied a great many minds. Competitors have contemplated his ceaseless movement with furrowed brows. Journalists and interviewers have generally retired bemused. Much quoted he may be, but Murdoch generally gives little away about what drives him so relentlessly forward.

"From my perspective, what drives him is that he wants to leave a mark. He honestly believes in the good the mass media does. It may sound high falutin, but he really does believe the media are the guarantors of democracy," his daughter, Elisabeth Murdoch, has said.[8] This does, indeed, sound high falutin. It is difficult to see how topless girls in the *Sun* or News Corp's market dominance in various media markets actually does good. The idea of Murdoch as the guarantor of democracy is paradoxical, to say the least.

Murdoch's longtime friend Irwin Stelzer has somewhat mysteriously observed: "I hate to say that money doesn't matter, because money always matters, but I think Rupert mainly sees himself as a kind of anti-Establishment revolutionary."[9] (Murdoch and Stelzer were actually next-door neighbors for a while but they found that they spent too much time working together.) Once again the idea that Murdoch is anti-Establishment is trotted out. Perhaps Murdoch does see himself as something of an outsider, a well-tailored rebel against the Establishment. It is a perception that bears little scrutiny under the harsh light of reality. Oxford-educated, right-wing media moguls are unlikely and largely unwilling revolutionaries. History suggests that there are few revolutionaries in pinstriped suits.

Finally, we are left with deep psychological theories about Murdoch's going one better than his father in creating a media empire or in pure desire for power. "You can demonize me by using the word *power*. But that's the fun of it, isn't it? Having a smidgen of power," Murdoch told biographer William Shawcross.[10]

Murdoch is such a chameleon that his various protestations may perhaps be taken with a pinch of salt. What can be said is that he is perpetually enthused by the range of possibilities and the sheer potential of his organization.

Murdoch's energy plays a crucial role in motivating others and in liberating energy in others. High performers like Murdoch discover energy from the mundane, from the routine. They extract ideas to generate enthusiasm. They invent different approaches and try new things. They generate energy from themselves and stimulate energy in those they work with. They attract people with energy.

The most obvious manifestation of these people's energy is their sheer enthusiasm. It is something they carefully cultivate and nurture, and it is highly infectious. Go to a Tom Peters seminar and even if you do not remember a single idea, you will

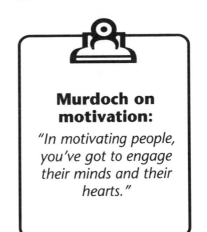

Murdoch on motivation:

"In motivating people, you've got to engage their minds and their hearts."

remember that Peters is an enthusiast who can transmit his enthusiasm so that people begin to believe in their own potential. Leaders transmit energy.

AMBITION NEVER DIES

♦ *Keep learning. Old dogs can, and must, learn new tricks. The skills and ideas utilized by Rupert Murdoch today are not those he utilized ten years ago or even one year ago. He is prepared to change and to learn.*

♦ *Keep questioning. "You have to expose yourself to your environment and ask questions to develop your sensitivity and sensibility," says Harvard's Ted Levitt. "I see things all the time. I go into factories, offices, stores and look out the window and just see things and ask, Why? Why are they doing that? Why are things this way and not that? You ask questions and pretty soon you come up with answers. When you begin to try to answer your own questions, you become much more receptive to reading things which help you to answer questions. Seeing is one thing but perception requires cognitive effort and personal involvement. You bring something to what you see."[12] Questioning is integral to how top managers add value to their organizations.*

♦ *Keep working. Even in his late eighties, Harold Geneen worked a ten-hour day at his office in New York's Waldorf-Astoria Hotel running Gunther International. "Putting deals together beats spending every day playing golf," he once said. Rupert Murdoch shows no signs of heading off to the nearest golf course.*

♦ *Keep making mistakes. "The great thing about television is that you can bury your mistakes quickly and move on to something new," says Murdoch.[13] The most powerful learning usually comes from your own mistakes.*

Murdoch himself has talked about his motivational style: "In motivating people, you've got to engage their minds and their hearts. I motivate people, I hope, by example—and perhaps by excitement, by having productive ideas to make others feel involved."[11]

NOTES

1 Ahmed, Kamal and Beavis, Simon, "Murdoch marriage break-up shakes media industry," *The Guardian*, April 22, 1998.

2 Parkes, Christopher and Newman, Cathy, "Dealmaker's dilemma," *Financial Times*, April 25–26, 1998.

3 Quoted in White, L., "Net prophet," *Sunday Times*, November 12, 1995.

4 "Background briefing," Australian Broadcasting Corporation, March 10, 1996.

5 Schendler, B., "Bill Gates and Paul Allen talk," *Fortune*, October 2, 1995.

6 "Background briefing," Australian Broadcasting Corporation.

7 Solomon, Norman, "Media moguls on board," *Think Tank Monitor*, January/February 1998.

8 Farhi, Paul, "Murdoch, all business," *Washington Post*, February 12, 1995.

9 Farhi, Paul, "Murdoch, all business."

10 Shawcross, William, *Murdoch*, Chatto & Windus, London, 1992.

11 Safire, William and Safire, Leonard, *Leadership: A Treasury of Great Quotations*, 1990.

12 Interview with Stuart Crainer, 1989.

13 "Background briefing," Australian Broadcasting Corporation.

10

Drive the Company

*The trouble with Rupert is that he operates with
his own set of rules.*

A COMPETITOR

CREATING EXCITEMENT

There is no escaping the fact that Murdoch presents a fearful specter for many who work for him, from the bottom of the organization to the very top. Scared people usually do what you want. There is undoubtedly an element of fear in Rupert Murdoch's management style. He is known by his initials KRM rather than by his name. He is not so personable as to be on first-name terms with his executives.

Yet you do not run a company worth billions of dollars and employing tens of thousands of people without being able to manage people effectively. This is a fact usually forgotten in discussions of Rupert Murdoch. His demonic reputation seems to preclude management. Yet tens of thousands of people work for him every day of the week. "The strange thing about Rupert Murdoch is not that people resign in protest at his methods. It is that hardly anyone does—even though he falls out with all his henchmen in the end," reflects former arts editor of the *Times*, Tim de Lisle.[1]

The assumption is that Murdoch motivates people through fear and fear alone. As we have seen, there is clearly an undercurrent of fear in the way Murdoch leads his organization. However, his approach to managing and motivating people is clearly more complex than that.

In any organization, managing to motivate people over a number of years poses a sizable problem. People become stale and demotivated. After a while, things tend to stay the same. Complacency inevitably sets in and torpor reigns. It is at this point that the company is probably at its most vulnerable to acquisition or declining performance.

Central to the motivation offered by Murdoch is that News Corp is an exciting place to work. It is in a state of constant change and development. To more traditional managers this would be a nightmare. To the kind of risk-taking, seat-of-the-pants manager Murdoch admires, News Corp offers constant challenge.

Murdoch has managed to create an organization that appears adept at managing change and changing itself. He drives the company forward. Often it appears that the eventual destination is unknown, but his belief seems to be the existential one that you are always nearer your goal by not keeping still.

He has achieved this partly through the constant acquisition of new companies. New blood and new cultures are constantly being brought into the Murdoch empire. People who are tired or bored at one part of the company can find a new challenge elsewhere. A noticeable Murdoch technique is to buy a company and then draft in a new cadre of his own managers from elsewhere in the News Corp group. This has twin benefits: It signals a new broom and provides a fresh challenge for the old stagers.

(It is also interesting to note that Murdoch is adept at welding entirely different cultures together. There is little coverage of any internal divisions within News Corp. Even those who have left have usually been silent on internal disagreements.)

Murdoch has managed to escape the complacency endemic in virtually all successful organizations. Part of the reason for this is that he has constantly been forging ahead in new markets or with entirely new products. Product launches are exciting events providing a motivation of their own. But they are always dangerous. "There is nothing more difficult to take in hand, more perilous to conduct, or more uncertain in its success, than to take the lead in the introduction of a new order of things," noted Machiavelli. Continually shaking things up is not easy. There are few examples of CEOs who have managed to inculcate an atmosphere of constant change over a significant period of time. Most introduce a short-lived period of change and then move on. Murdoch has kept the ball rolling, eschewing complacency. This has assured the success of his company and provided a ready source of motivation for executives.

Murdoch has also followed one of Machiavelli's other suggestions on the behavior of the leader. "He ought above all things to keep his men well-organized and drilled, to follow incessantly the chase," wrote the Florentine diplomat. The momentum created by making acquisitions and seizing new opportunities means that Murdoch's executives rarely sit still and take stock. The next challenge is always just around the corner.

CHANGE ADDS VALUE

Murdoch realizes that driving the company to change itself continually is the way forward. Change adds value at an individual and organizational level.

Murdoch keeps News Corp young at heart. It displays little of the torpor typical of many huge organizations. Young companies are the chief source of dynamic growth in the economy. Annual sales revenues from *Fortune 500* companies once accounted for 60 percent of U.S. GDP. By 1994 this had been reduced to 35 percent. Interestingly, in 1994 the 500 ranked companies employed 11.6 million people—a figure almost identical to that of 1965.[2]

If the same number of people generate less sales than they did 30 years ago, where is corporate growth to come from? Thomas Doorley of Braxton Associates observes that a mere 200 companies accounted for 11 percent of all jobs created in the U.S. during the last decade. These include some familiar names—Microsoft and Wal-Mart—and many unfamiliar ones. Dynamic upstarts are the source of growth. (And yet, 80 percent of businesses fail in the first five years.)

In response, Braxton Associates has developed a "Growth System"—"a three-step process helps restart stalled growth engines as well as sustaining value-creating growth." First, this requires a commitment to growth (less common than it sounds, but an automatic reflex for someone like Murdoch). Second, firms need to execute actions across the three phases of growth (create a "valuable formula," exploit the formula and manage the transition to the next phase of formula creation). Third, successful companies build foundations of leadership, organizational architecture, culture, processes and knowledge to sustain growth.

Beyond the jargon the message is simple—companies that grow change constantly and avoid complacency.

There is some irony in the fact that the anti-theoretical Murdoch is actually a mirror image of managerial best practice. One of the leading strategic thinkers of recent years is Gary Hamel, coauthor of the best-selling *Competing for the Future*.[3] Hamel presents a blueprint of the characteristics of the contemporary master of strategy—and gives an idea of why Murdoch is so successful.

First, the general rules: "A company surrenders today's businesses when it gets smaller faster than it gets better. A company surrenders tomorrow's businesses when it gets better without getting different," says Hamel.

The chief means of avoiding surrender is through avoiding grinding to a halt. Corporate strategists have got to keep the momentum going. "In many companies you see institutional entropy. How do you teach individuals to be enemies of entropy? It is like being a map maker in an earthquake zone. We are talking about products entering a market which is emerging and changing. How do you create strategy in the absence of a map?" says Hamel. This is an area in which Murdoch is unquestionably a master. He is willing to move forward and, crucially, he is willing to make mistakes.

Murdoch continually challenges traditional assumptions. "The motto of Fox Sports pretty much sums up the nature of our Fox network," he says. "Perhaps it's the motto, or should be the motto, of our whole company: Same game, new attitude."[4]

As Gary Hamel argues, it is only by challenging convention that change will happen. "Taking risks,

breaking the rules, and being a maverick have always been important, but today they are more crucial than ever. We live in a discontinuous world—one where digitalization, deregulation and globalization are profoundly reshaping the industrial landscape," he says.[5] Murdoch is one of those reshaping the industrial world. This is reflected in the common observation—usually by competitors—that he plays by a completely different set of rules than anyone else.

Murdoch also fits in with Hamel's thinking in a number of other ways. Hamel argues that there are three kinds of companies. First are "the real makers," companies such as British Airways and Xerox. They are the aristocracy; well-managed, consistent high achievers. Second, says Hamel, are the takers, "peasants who only keep what the Lord doesn't want." This group typically has around 15 percent market share—such as Kodak in the copier business or Avis. Avis' slogan, *"We try harder,"* enshrined the peasantry in its mission statement. "Harder doesn't get you anywhere," says Hamel dismissively.

Third are the breakers, the industrial revolutionaries. These are companies Hamel believes are creating the new wealth, and include the likes of Starbucks which is creating new wealth in the coffee business. "Companies should be asking themselves, who is going to capture the new wealth in your industry?" he says. Murdoch's News Corp clearly figures among the new wealth creators. It is not a bit player, second in an obscure market niche. It is at center stage, shaping new markets. "The primary agenda is to be the architect of industry transformation, not simply corporate transformation," says Hamel. Companies that view change as an internal matter are liable to be left behind. Instead they need to look outside of their industry boundaries. Hamel calculates that if you want to see the future coming, 80 percent of the learning will take place outside company boundaries. Looking outside is not something companies are very good at. "The good news is that companies in most industries are blind in the same way," says Hamel. "There is no inevitability about the future. There is no proprietary data about the future. The goal is to imagine what you can make happen."

Hamel argues that there are four preconditions for wealth-creating strategies. It is intriguing here that while Murdoch and News Corp closely fit many of Hamel's other ideas, they fare less well when Hamel turns to how these things can be achieved. First, Hamel says that a company must have "new passions." People inside the organization must care deeply about the future. Strategy has to rediscover passion. This is true to some extent with News Corp.

Second, wealth creation requires "new voices." In many companies Hamel observes "a lack of genetic diversity. Young people are largely disenfranchised from discussions of strategy. We need a hierarchy of imagination, not experience. Among the people who work on strategy in organizations and the theorists, a huge proportion, perhaps 95 percent, are economists and engineers who share a mechanistic view of strategy. Where are the theorists, the anthropologists to give broader and fresher insights?"

Third, Hamel calls for "new conversations." Instead of having the same five people talking to the same five people for the fifth year in a row, more people need to become involved in the process of strategy creation.

Finally, there is a need for "new perspectives." "You cannot make people any smarter but you can give them new lenses," says Hamel. "Only nonlinear strategies will create new wealth."

These final factors are not evident in Murdoch's domination of News Corp. There is no suggestion of more than a handful of people being involved in shaping the company's future. The future and strategies to make the most of it are in Murdoch's hands and in his imagination.

DRIVE THE COMPANY

♦ *Change is the route to success. A becalmed company is dead in the water. Murdoch drives News Corp forever forward. You are always closer to your goal by not keeping still.*

♦ *Stay young at heart. Small companies are the source of dynamism within industrial economies. Any large organization that manages to retain the entrepreneurial freshness of youth will succeed.*

♦ *Cultivate revolution. Revolution is the way to fame and fortune. Inventing markets is more lucrative and powerful than entering markets.*

NOTES

1   de Lisle, Tim, "Something had to go: me," *The Guardian*, March 2, 1998.

2   Doorley, Thomas, "Real growth, real value," *Worldlink*, March/April 1996.

3   Hamel, Gary, and Prahalad, C. K., *Competing for the Future*, Harvard Business School Publishing, 1996.

4   "Background briefing," Australian Broadcasting Corporation, March 10, 1996.

5   Hamel, Gary, "Killer strategies that make shareholders rich," *Fortune*, June 23, 1997.

How to Succeed Like Rupert Murdoch

1. Start early

There is no substitute for getting your hands dirty early on.

2. Move with the times

Ideas develop and evolve—so, too, must yours.

3. Have faith in yourself and your business; nothing else

Leave theories to the theorists. Let the politicians keep their ideals. Business is action, nothing more.

4. Network

Constantly update and develop your network of contacts. Network widely among politicians, business-people and thought leaders. You are who you know.

5. Be ruthless and fair

Manage people like corporate assets: tough and straight.

6. Play hard

Backtracking is weakness. Stand your ground.

7. Compete to win

You get no medals for coming in second.

8. Play the long game

Accept short-term pain for long-term gain.

9. Move fast

"Unlike his competitors, Mr. Murdoch acts quickly," noted one article.[1]

10. Ask questions

"Established companies are constantly preoccupied with how they need to compete in their business without ever questioning the who and the what of their business," laments London Business School's Costas Markides.[2] Questions lead to tomorrow's strategic answers.

11. Lead from the front

Set an example, but choose your example with care.

12. Envision the future

Take time out from the present to invent the future.

13. Forego management bullshit

No mission statements. No fancy jargon. No consultants.

---

14. Believe in yourself

Rupert Murdoch has huge internal reservoirs of self-confidence. He knows what he wants and what he is capable of.

15. Embrace the world

A deal is a deal, no matter where. Murdoch was a global manager before the concept was widely practiced or understood.

16. Embrace technology

Forget technobabble and nerdishness; technology creates markets and creates economies of production and delivery.

17. Keep learning

Learn new tricks, even if you are an old dog.

18. Make mistakes

Murdoch missed out on cable TV, preferring satellite broadcasting. He learns.

19. Create fear

"I would simply not count Murdoch out of anything, prima facie," said an investment banker. Competitors fear Murdoch. He makes that work to his benefit.

20. Take risks

Life and business demand that we take risks to succeed.

NOTES

1   Gove, Alex, "Lord of the skies," *Red Herring*, Issue 44, July 1997.

2   Markides, Constantinos, "Strategic innovation: the leaders' dilemma," *Sloan Management Review*, Spring 1998.

Will News Corp Survive?

S pring 1998 provided a poignant example of corporate mortality. In April, *New York Post* gossip columnist Liz Smith wrote: "It is with some personal sadness that I announce the amicable separation of Rupert Murdoch and his beautiful wife, Anna, after 32 years of marriage and three children. The Murdochs say their situation is very painful and leaves them torn, but they are attempting to work out their differences. Mrs. Murdoch, a novelist and philanthropist, will remain on the board and continue in the Murdoch businesses." Later, Anna Murdoch filed for divorce in California. News Corp shares fell as analysts and investors contemplated the long-term future of Rupert Murdoch, his wife and children, and News Corp.

Anna Murdoch is a main board director of News Corp and no simple corporate wife. She is a novelist who has, with Murdochian efficiency, turned some of her husband's career into fiction. Anna Murdoch's

1988 novel was entitled *Family Business*. It tells the story of a media mogul and his family. The family self-destructs amid civil war about succeeding the mogul.

Whether dynastic civil war is likely is a matter of debate. Murdoch has a "dynastic obsession," according to ex-*Sunday Times* editor Andrew Neil.

Like his father before him, it is likely that Rupert Murdoch would like to leave a sizable media empire as his tombstone. Sir Keith Murdoch failed to leave a substantial business. His son would appear to be in a hugely superior position to do so.

Murdoch's son Lachlan is chairman and managing director of News Ltd., the Australian side of the empire. Lachlan graduated from Princeton and is now officially the leader in waiting. Two of Murdoch's other children are also senior executives. Elisabeth is a senior exec at BSkyB. James Murdoch was made deputy publisher of the *New York Post* at the beginning of 1998. Previous to that he was president of News America Digital Publishing. Perhaps most mysterious is why and how three of Murdoch's children are so keen on following in his footsteps.

Doubts remain about the likely longevity of a Murdoch-less News Corporation. The fact is that the company has few of the characteristics of a long-term survivor.

In his book *The Living Company*, Arie de Geus says that long-lived companies are "sensitive to their environment"; "cohesive, with a strong sense of identity"; "tolerant"; and "conservative in financing."[1]

Key to de Geus' entire argument is that there is more to companies—and to longevity—than mere money making. "The dichotomy between profits and longevity is false," he says. His logic is impeccably straightforward. Capital is no longer king; the skills, capabilities and knowledge of people are. The corollary from this is that "a successful company is one that can learn effectively." Learning is tomorrow's capital. In de Geus' eyes, learning means being prepared to accept continuous change.

Here, de Geus provides the new deal: Contemporary corporate man or woman must understand that the corporation will, and must, change and it can only change if its community of people changes also. Individuals must change and the way they change is through learning.

Similarly, Noel Tichy of the University of Michigan has argued that, "Effective leaders recognize that the ultimate test of leadership is sustained success, which demands the constant cultivation of future leaders."[2] Leaders must therefore invest in developing the leaders of tomorrow and they must communicate directly with those who will follow in their footsteps.

Tichy cites a number of American examples. Larry Bossidy, CEO of AlliedSignal, put all the company's 86,000 employees through a development program and managed to speak to 15,000 of them during his first year in the job. Along the way, Bossidy also increased the market value of the company by 400 percent in six years. Other exemplars are the usual suspects, including Andy Grove of Intel, GE's Jack Welch and Lew Platt of Hewlett-Packard.

Tichy believes that being able to pass on leadership skills to others requires three things. First, a "teachable point of view"—"You must be able to talk clearly and convincingly about who you are, why you exist and how you operate." Second, the leader requires a story. "Dramatic storytelling is the way people learn from one another," Tichy writes, suggesting that this explains why Bill Gates and the like feel the need to write books. The third element in passing on the torch of leadership is teaching methodology. "To be a great teacher you have to be a great learner." The great corporate leaders are hungry to know more and do not regard their knowledge as static or comprehensive.

Corporate longevity is perhaps the final and greatest test. With its capacity for change, News Corp appears well placed. Yet its Achilles' heel remains the source of so much of its inspiration: Keith Rupert Murdoch. He drives and cajoles the company forward in a way that means that his successors may have an impossible job on their hands.

NOTES

1   deGeus, Arie, *The Living Company*, Harvard Business School Publishing, 1997.
2   Tichy, Noel M., "The mark of a winner," *Leader to Leader*, Fall 1997.

Further Reading

Arrogant Aussie: The Rupert Murdoch Story, Michael Leapman, Lyle Stuart Inc., Syracuse, NY, 1984.

Citizen Murdoch, Thomas Kiernan, Dodd Mead & Co., New York, 1986.

Murdoch, William Shawcross, Simon & Schuster, New York, 1992.

A Paper Prince, George Munster, Viking, New York, 1984.

Rupert Murdoch, Jerome Tuccille, Donald I. Fine Inc., New York, 1989.

Index